# A little red book about source

Liberating management and living life with source principles

AQUILAE EDITIONS
Place de Boccard 10
CH-1762 Givisiez, Switzerland
aquilae@ordinata.ch
www.aquilae-editions.ch

**Order this book at www.alittleredbookaboutsource.com**, on the main Internet platforms, or from your bookseller.
Source stories at: www.alittleredbookaboutsource.com
To contact the author: stefan.merckelbach@ordinata.ch

Print: ISBN 978-2-940678-00-6
E-Book: ISBN 978-2-940678-01-3

First published under the title: *Un petit livre rouge sur la source*, Aquilae Editions 2019.

© 2020 Aquilae Editions, Ordinata, Ltd.

Stefan Merckelbach

# A little red book about source

Liberating management and living life
with source principles

Afterword by Peter John Koenig
Photography by Vincent Delfosse

1ˢᵗ English Edition
Translated from the French by Karen Smith

AQUILAE EDITIONS
2020

# Contents

*On the threshold*
Beginner's mind    11

*I. Meeting source*
1. Who's a source?    17
2. The source person's work    25
3. Recognizing yourself as source and living it out    41

*II. Sharing source*
4. Sources—global and specific    59
5. The source develops the collective    73
6. Seeing the source in each person    85

*III. Transmitting source*
7. When the time is ripe, pass it on    99
8. Transmitting source, step-by-step    111
9. Cast your bread upon the waters    129

## Epilogue
Principles of love     135

## Afterword by Peter John Koenig
Changing times     141

## Vincent Delfosse
Images and words of source     145

## Acknowledgements
Another source adventure     149

## Resources
Source principles—first sightings in print     153
Reading notes     155
Trainings and consulting on source principles     160

## Index
161

"The water is turbid from its source"
*Persian proverb*

"The poet can only create when the god is within him"
*Epitaph of* Norbert Moret, composer

"What counts, it dawned on me, is not only *what* leaders do and *how* they do it, but that 'interior condition', the *inner place* from which they operate."
Otto Scharmer, *Theory U*

# On the threshold

## *Beginner's mind*

---

**C**URIOUS about the title of "The Source Person" training day, on 25 September 2013 I innocently turned up, completely clueless as to just how much this experience would transform my professional life and my organization. Although only three participants were registered, Peter John Koenig, the moderator, surprised us by deciding to hold the day-long workshop anyway. A stroke of luck for us, as we got his full attention—just as he had ours. A long-time Swiss resident from London, his shock of white hair signalled that he was close to retirement age, but the energy in his bright eyes and his vivid presentation of the "source principles" made it abundantly clear that retiring was the farthest thing from his mind. Based on what I discovered that day I signed up for a longer program, a master class he organized the next year to transmit his findings. Since then the notion of source has become integral to the support and training we provide at

Ordinata, a company I started in 2001. Our team is highly motivated to spread the source principles far and wide, beginning with every aspect of our own work. By now, it's become unthinkable for us to work with a client and not delve into the question of source. Each new exploration validates and deepens our understanding of these principles. The little red book you hold in your hands (or follow on your screen) is the fruit of these experiences.

If you ask Peter Koenig where the source principles came from, he'll say they are as old as the world. He didn't invent them himself but just watched the ways other people grappled with the projects in their lives, and then exchanged views with them on the process. But as old as these principles may be, Peter Koenig is clearly the source of their uncovering: it was he who first developed the vocabulary that makes sense out of these patterns, the language you will encounter in these pages. Starting his research in the 1980's, he spoke about it publicly from 2000 on, and in 2009 he began to give presentations on source principles in Quebec, Brussels and Berlin. At first he just wanted to exchange ideas and compare notes with others on best practices, but before long it became clear that their experiences were so similar to his own that the emerging patterns in fact could be seen as principles. These days his ongoing research on source is being amplified in an international network of contributors (www.workwithsource.com*), which I'm a member of.

As yet, not much has been written on the theme of source (see the very meagre Resources section at the end of this book). What you'll read here is based on my own regular conversations with Peter Koenig about

*The asterisk (\*) refers to an entry in the Resources section at the end of the book (153).*

his work, and on years of provocative trainings, reflection days and follow-up exchanges with fellow master class participants. My Ordinata colleagues, who've made the source a central theme in their work, have been an indispensable fountain of source insights, as has my long-time collaboration with Martine Marenne on "participatory dynamics". Personal interviews with Peter Koenig gave me direct access to the source of the source principles, and I'm deeply grateful to him for his availability, enduring kindness, and careful reading and revision of the manuscript.

Now that you know something about how this idea of source emerged, you're probably eager to find out what it means. In the following pages, I invite you to explore the theme of source in three stages, and to follow the natural flow of discovering what source means and how its principles can be adopted. First we'll try to understand what source is about so we can give it a warm welcome, then we'll consider how to share it with other people, and finally in what way, when the time is right, to pass it on. But now let's stop the preliminaries and start our voyage of discovery.

One last thing: why is this little book red? I'll tell you all about it in the epilogue.

## Part One
# MEETING SOURCE

# Chapter 1

## *Who's a source?*

A SOURCE is a person who has taken an initiative and through that has become the source of something: we can call this a "source person". We take initiatives all the time: deciding on a particular course of study, going after a certain job, starting up a business, planning a special dinner. I can initiate a friendship or partnership, change my housing situation, make holiday plans, decide to have a child. Or I might step forward to join a project sourced by someone else. But whatever the undertaking, every time I take an initiative, I am setting something in motion that has not yet been switched on. At that moment I become the source, or source person, of my initiative.

In the beginning, before that moment, there had been an idea, an intuition, an inspiration. I listened to these prompts before my initiative took on a definite shape, and brought them on board. As a source person, although I took the initiative in the first place, I didn't in fact originate it: instead, the idea came to me, the intuition occurred, all of a sudden the inspiration arose. Ideas are gifts. It might look like it was my idea, my intuition, my inspiration—and in a way that's true because I'm the one who made the gift my own. It definitely took form within me, and I'm also the one who expressed it and communicated it. But it's not mine in the sense of belonging to me, it's something I've received. The source person adopts an attitude of humility about his idea, being aware that he is its repository, not its owner. This is crucial and we will come back to it.

To be the source, or source person, I don't have to generate the original idea myself—it can come from someone else. Some enormously creative individuals in this world come up with a new idea every minute, but they don't automatically become a source until they take the initiative to launch the *realisation* of the idea. Even if the idea person himself doesn't switch it on, he can inspire somebody else to run with the idea (this is another way to receive it) and initiate the enterprise. In this case it's this later person, and not the idea's originator, who is the source person.

The image of a spring bubbling up from the earth's depths is relevant here—the water doesn't spontaneously surge forth out of nothing, it comes from somewhere. Recognizing this principle is already a way of respecting it. When I take up an idea not actually fabricated by me (though it comes directly through me), and take the initiative to make it happen, make it concrete, make it exist in the world—even if I frequently rely on others to help me get it going—that's when I cross the threshold

to become source or source person. In other words, source designates a person who takes an initiative based on an idea he or she has taken on.

Luckily for the source person the idea (which is a gift in itself) comes with another reward: the energy needed to take the initiative. It's as if the original idea's line of communication—which Peter Koenig calls the "source channel", also channels the rising sap needed to transform the idea into reality. This energy wells up from deep within the person, igniting his strengths and filling him with the capacity to take action, if he so decides by an act of his free will, to incorporate the idea, welcome the energy and set the process in motion.

There are basically two ways of being source or source person: taking an initiative for something completely new (in which case you're the "global source" of the initiative) or joining up with someone else's initiative (which makes you a "specific source" of the initiative). We'll return to this in chapter 4, but for now the point is that in both situations—even though the idea was a gift—you are the source of your own presence within the initiative: your participation is an authentic expression of your freedom, your power to act, and your creativity.

Let's take an example. Looking for a job, Jayden answers an ad and gets an interview. The company is the source of the ad, and Jayden is the source of the job application and of coming to the interview (nobody made him do it). The company's recruiter is the source of a concrete job offer, while Jayden is the source of his response. If he accepts it, let's hope he can quickly become the source of his new position—that is, be someone who listens to his intuition and takes initiatives to develop his job in line with the mission he's accepted.

For Jayden, progressively becoming the source person of his new job would mean

- to employ his power to act, doing so in line with the company's overall frame of reference, to take full possession of the position's responsibilities and scope of decision-making;
- supported by his intuitions, to exercise his freedom and creativity to find new ways of developing his mandate—which gives rise to new initiatives;
- to experience his source as a strong motivation or passion, until he's convinced it's time to pass on his source to someone else and invest his own passion elsewhere.

In the following chapters we'll deepen our understanding of what it means to be the source or source person of your work, roles and functions; the scope of your responsibilities and relationships; your projects and what you own or have use of—with the aim of more fully living out your role as source person. But before we go any further, some clarifications. As Peter Koenig does, we will distinguish between source, source person, and source principles.

A **source person** takes an initiative based on an idea.

**Source** can be understood in one of two ways:

- From the standpoint of the person doing the sourcing (the *subject*), source is synonymous with source person—the person who takes the initiative. The word "source" specifically expresses the role the person plays in relation to his initiative (this is Peter Koenig's general use of the term).

- From the standpoint of the thing being sourced (the *object*), source can also designate the heart of the initiative, the essence of that which the individual is the source person of—that is, the vision and values that constitute the deep core of his initiative (no matter whether it's a function, a relationship, a home or a project). Source is, in a sense, the *source* of the source person. This vision and these values are transmitted by one source person to another by passing along the role of source—the way a baton in a relay race is passed along. Putting yourself in contact with this interior core, joining with it and staying connected with it throughout the implementation of the initiative, is exactly what Peter Koenig means by welcoming one's source.

Finally, **source principles** refer to the phenomena that characterize both the activities of the source person (the *subject* who sets something in motion), and the implementation of the source itself (the deep core of the *object* which the initiative sets in motion). Over the course of his research, Peter Koenig observed some consistent patterns in the way people successfully exercise source, and certain pitfalls it would be better to avoid.

As a whole, these patterns, along with observations on the source's or source person's function, are referred to here as "source principles".

Now that the terms are clear, for the rest of this book I gladly leave out the quotation marks around source, source person, and source principles.

As the source principles will demonstrate, the source person is always a specific person: a "he" or a "she". To reflect the fact that these principles do not privilege one gender over another, from chapter to chapter I'll change the personal pronouns designating sources.

# Chapter 2

## *The source person's work*

UNDERSTANDING what the words mean is an indispensable first step, but the real challenge is putting them into effect. All the more so for the source person, whose role is explicitly defined by taking an initiative that chiefly consists of setting actions in motion. Instead of standing paralysed in the face of her idea, the source person gets things going to make her initiative happen. She has something to accomplish—the ancient Greeks called this task an *ergon*, meaning an item of work, an action, a *doing* that flows into an output. It's like a work of art by a poet or painter. For a source person, her *ergon* is both an implementation path (the work) and the work's result (the output). But the source person's work is more complex than a simple fabrication. Unlike mechanically following an instruction manual or putting an Ikea bed together, it requires setting a course, making adjustments according to the ups and downs of the experience, and continually aligning the implementation with the chosen course. As a result, the source person's action is both very strong and very fragile. A formidable surge propels the source person to undertake, develop and complete her initiative, but the undertaking is also very delicate. It is constantly susceptible to being buffeted by unpredictable and unmanageable circumstances, and to being influenced by her own imperfections as a source person. To move her initiative forward, she learns not only to explore the power of her actions, but also to grapple with their inherent weaknesses, and to address her own shortcomings.

So what exactly does this work, this *ergon*, consist of? The source person's three main tasks correlate with her three main roles:

1. To actualize the intuitions (ideas, vision) she receives, the source person initiates actions and undertakes risks. This is the role of source as entrepreneur.

2. The source person launches her initiative into the future—an arc that continues throughout its evolution. She does this by constantly clarifying, and then communicating, the next steps to be taken. This is the source's role as guide.

3. The source person ensures that the project's framework—its values and vision—is respected. This is the source's role as guardian.

Let's look at these three roles, and their corresponding tasks, a little more closely.

**1. The source person as entrepreneur.** As explained in the previous chapter, the source person is someone who takes an initiative based on an idea. Peter Koenig notes that throughout the life of an initiative, the source person continues to receive ideas, insights, inspirations, and the energy to make them happen. We may now add the dimension of risk-taking, which inevitably accompanies the initiative—itself more or less a dive into the unknown. At every source person's core there lies a bold "fool", whose faith in her initiative can overflow the limits of what's reasonable. She seems to cloak herself with a certain naiveté, or as Mark Twain might have put it, she didn't know it was impossible, that's why she did it! Taking risks is crucial to her role as an entrepreneur: if she can't take risks, she becomes an obstacle and handicaps her initiative.

Looking back over my twenty years as the source of Ordinata, it appears that risk, or lack of it, has correlated with periods of development and stagnation. Initiatives taken during the company's development phases have been accompanied or even triggered by taking risks, while periods of stagnation have all been characterized by not doing so. Realizing this in hindsight has been a great help in resuming the risk taking when needed. Having lived through the interconnections between initiative, risk and development, I can say that a company's greatest risk is… to stop taking risks. Lack of risk-taking will certainly hasten the enterprise's decline, even where there are other contributing factors.

Risk is not a goal in itself, and has no inherent value as such, but by allowing the initiative to meander into unknown and untried realms, it does *add* value. An initiative is a beginning. It always leads to something new—if not in itself, at least for the person who launches it. Risk is the price of admission into what is new. In this sense, risk is more like an investment, and any entrepreneur knows that to earn something you must first invest. This explains why a cash-rich company can appear healthy when it's actually in crisis: the company's resources are being allowed to sleep instead of revving up for its future.

The source person's risk is not only financial: she can also risk her reputation, for example, or a promotion, or even her job, just as she can risk the future of a relationship, or her health, or the very roof over her head. Taking a risk also expresses the source person's trust in her initiative. It's a testimonial to the project, and her confidence benefits all the other people who are working to achieve it. But above all, her trust in the project helps her muster the courage to take the next step.

As a source person trying to advance my initiative, I regularly ask myself, "Am I still risking enough for this project?"

**2. The source person as guide.** From the very first step of a new initiative springs a series of follow-up steps. As a guide, the source person's role is to make sure her initiative doesn't wither on the vine, but stays vital and develops to fruition. Let's distinguish the first initiative, the gateway initiative that starts a new project, from the spectrum of subsequent initiatives taken to develop the project throughout its evolution. As a matter of fact, while the first initiative engenders the project (by taking a new job, starting a new business, creating a neighbourhood association, proposing marriage, buying a boat), the initiatives that follow are necessary in developing the project and letting it flourish according to its original purpose.

From there, each next step contributes to the future form of the project, and each new initiative (whether it comes from the source person, other project participants, or a combination of the two) will have to align with this flow. In the end, it's up to the source person to guide the process. In bringing it to life, she's already exercised her role as entrepreneur, and now she will take on the role of guide by setting course for the first of many landmarks. There's nothing unusual about this: it's perfectly natural for the painter who draws a preliminary sketch to keep working on his canvas until the painting is finished, and the same goes for the source person who, by calling the project into being, legitimately presides over its deployment. As source, she has to do this herself: no one can do it for her.

This guiding role consists in giving direction to the ongoing cascade of initiatives meant to achieve the project's vision and ensure its sustainability. The source person as guide has two tasks: to clarify what the next step is, and then to communicate it to those who will contribute to realizing it. Clarifying the next step is far from easy, not least because the

source person often has no idea what that step should be. Sometimes, it may just be a question of tranquilly considering the possibilities until clarity arises. But paradoxically for a guide, the source person is more frequently hampered by a fog of indecision, stumbling around blindly trying to evaluate the options. Unsure of her own judgement, she procrastinates, longing for a bit more information. Anxious about the consequences of a wrong move, she paralyses herself and gets depressed… etcetera. Welcome to the Source Club! It's perfectly normal to doubt yourself—any source person will testify to this. The source person is just like you and me—she's not a magician or a superhero, and very far from divine: trying to guide while groping in the dark isn't easy for anyone.

To get clear on what the next step is, the source person has access to three effective tools: she can listen to her own intuitions, reflect on her insights, and turn outwards to engage in dialogue with others. Let's see how this works.

As a guide, the source person instinctively puts a high value on *intuition*.* Back when she took the first step as entrepreneur, wasn't she already obliged to trust her intuition? On the strength of her initial experience, throughout the life of the project she continues to pay attention to new ideas, inspirations, and visions. But intuitions are gifts, and their arrival can't be controlled. Even so, as a source person you can take actions that promote them: temporarily hitting the pause button, taking some silent breathing space in nature or a moment of prayer, giving yourself some time out to play sports, take a hike or even have a quick shower. Altered states, those times you find yourself staring vacantly into the middle distance, can encourage intuitions to emerge, but this doesn't necessarily mean that the next step will suddenly become clear. For that to happen we need powers that are easier for a source person to operate, techniques that can really deliver clarity about the next step.

One of these means is *reflection*, a pause when the source person takes time alone to put her thoughts in order. She takes time for herself (she might even want to book a date in her agenda) to advance her understanding of the step that must be taken next to develop her project. For the source person, it's a time of re-sourcing, when she reconnects with her own source channel* and focuses on preparations for the next step. As with intuition, it's helpful to create the right conditions: to foster this reflective process, find a spot that inspires you and provides supportive circumstances where you can concentrate. And definitely don't suppose that when you're sitting on a bench in the forest you're not working. A guilty conscience has no place here: you're never working as hard, nor as productively for your project as when you're taking care of your main role—that of source person. In my life, to make sure I don't neglect this important means of gathering information I put these solo meetings in my agenda and call them "source time".

The other great means of clarification is *dialogue*. Let's remember we're fundamentally all relationship beings, and the source person is no different. Lacking clarity about the next step, she naturally turns to other people to discuss it, raise questions, ask for feedback and advice, produce objections, and think together about the next step. This dialogue, which is a sharing of the source person's own reflective approach, takes the form of a one-to-one conversation, a group discussion, or both, and can be done repeatedly to get a range of opinions. Group dialogue benefits from the amplifying effect of *collective intelligence*: one person's remark inspires another person to weigh in on it, which resonates with a third person, and so on, so that the final outcome is greater than just the sum of the individual reflections. Having a dialogue doesn't mean the source person has to adopt everybody else's views—but listening to them enriches her own vision of the situation, getting a clearer and clearer picture of what needs to be done to take the project to the next level. Dialogue promotes nuanced distinctions, which is a source of renewal. It keeps us from getting stuck in the way we've always done it and lets us move forward to take the next step. While intuition is instantaneous and involves only the source person, mediation through dialogue is relatively slow, a process in which the next step reveals itself only gradually in the source person's mind. Through interactions with others, at one point she realizes that the fog has completely dissipated—and her doubts with it. She now knows what the next step is. This next step might involve a certain risk; by becoming aware of it, she puts her guide's role at the service of her entrepreneur's role.

Once she's achieved clarity, the source person engages in the second guiding task: *communicating the clarity* she's gained through dialogue, reflection and intuition. She talks about it with those who are either working on the project with her or who will be affected by the next step in some way, and explains how it makes sense for the project. Peter Koenig points out that to get others to follow her lead, the source doesn't really have to do anything except communicate this clarity. Her collaborators are not obliged to unquestioningly follow her advice—remember, in the dialogue phase they've already expressed their diverging opinions at length. Rather, in terms of the project's overall vision (they've subscribed to it ever since they freely joined up in the first place) the source's clarity about the next step makes sense to them. I've seen this in a wide array of companies and institutions: the moment the source person expresses herself unambiguously, the other people's approval follows naturally—and this is true even if her proposed next step doesn't seem entirely reasonable. Moreover, it's impressive to see how, along with her clarity, the source person communicates the energy they will require to help her make it happen. It's as if she is bestowing energy she gets from her own source channel, and that a spark of her passion for the project is transferred to them, firing up their own motivation.

But what happens when a source person doesn't feel confident as a communicator? In this case, she can rely on someone else's capacities, all the while exercising control over what's being communicated. This someone else, as Peter Koenig notes, will often be the project's number two person.

**3. The source person as guardian.** As we've seen above, the source person's role as guide is based on intuition, reflection and dialogue with others. In her guide role, she nurtures the initiative's development, while as guardian she ensures that, along the course of its development, it doesn't lose its soul.

While in her role as guide she gradually fine-tunes the actual next steps of the project, as a guardian she sketches the big picture and maintains a birds-eye view. When a source person takes the first initiative in a new project—the one that launches it—she's moving it forward, driven by an idea, an intuition, an inspiration. As the idea ramifies, the source develops a *vision* of how to proceed toward the overarching goals of the project (the *purpose*, intention, objective—the result in terms of "what" and "why"). She sees the main thrust and chief means of getting there (this is the *pathway*, the itinerary, the "how"). The vision—both the purpose and the pathway—functions like a red margin line for the project, leading it forward and conserving its parameters, mainly for the source person herself but also for all those who, in one role or another, will participate in it. But this red line—much like the red thread guiding the way through a labyrinth—is not carved in stone. It can and often must evolve in one way or another: to properly guard the course of the project (the purpose), it's obvious that the source person must make adjustments to the process and the means (the pathway). And all the more so when significant changes appear unexpectedly in the project environment.

The importance of this guiding thread is shown in a recent Swiss example. When new legislation made (previously discretionary) canine obedience courses obligatory for new dog owners, dog training enterprises scrambled to adapt the way they did business. A few years later the law was repealed, so they had to adapt back to the way it had been before the upheaval. Judging by the obedience school where Athos (our dog) has become a regular, these legal fluctuations have not shaken its main purpose: the enterprise's source person has successfully adapted the project's pathway (the how) to the changing circumstances, all the while keeping its focus on the essential what and why.

It must be understood that no one but the source person herself can change the project's vision. Although she may use dialogue, intuition and reflection to clarify adjustments (these could be seen as "next steps" for the project), no one can coerce her to change the project's vision. On the other hand, being the sole person with the power to modify the vision comes with the great responsibility to see it through when necessary for the good of the project.

The soul of the project, its essential core, is expressed not only through the source person's vision, but also through *values*. These values play a key role, something like traffic cones for everybody's conduct in the project, or guard rails for their actions. The values provide inspiration for concrete everyday behaviours—in fact, the values that came with the source person's initiative will be a blueprint for how to get things done in the project. This is illustrated by one source person, a client of ours from the industry sector, who designated velocity as one of his company's values. Far from being an eccentric choice, for him this value reflected a need for fast reaction times in a demanding and constantly changing market. The actions of every single person—from the engineers to the administrators, from the workers to the researchers, from the director to the cleaning staff—were obliged to embody the same values of speed and agility that the source person had always associated with his company: it had to be speedy in order to survive.

Values express the institutional culture—whether explicitly articulated or implicitly perceived, they stick like glue, and are integral to the company or project. And crucially, these values are *the source person's* values. It's her task to engrave them onto the initiative's DNA, from where they continue to inspire her collaborators' actions throughout the life of the project—because the source person attracts to her project people who share those values. So does the source person just graft her own personal values onto her project? That's one possibility. She can also invite members of her group to formulate the values along with her (a way of dialoguing with them)—but this only makes sense if the source person can be perfectly satisfied with the outcome. In other words, if she can be assured that the terms formulated in the group correspond to what she herself sees as the project's values. It can also happen that the source person isn't convinced that the project's values originated with her, but feels they were already embedded in the idea, intuition, inspiration she had at the beginning. So in this case, all she had to do from then on was go along with them. But no matter how the values become part of the project, it's *always* the source person who acknowledges what they are, injects them visibly into the project, and cares for them by making sure they are respected by everyone.

In light of this dynamic, Peter Koenig warns us about so-called shared values. If the members of the collective do join the source person in formulating the project's values, it's not to agree on a sort of lowest common denominator, and then pat themselves on the back for making a group decision. If the project's values are "shared", it's not because everybody feels the same way about them. It's because they are the *project's* values (which are the source person's values), and because the people who chose to join the project resonated with these values, since those project values corresponded to their own. In other words, the source person and the members of the collective fundamentally "share" the same values not because they defined them together, but because they've already resonated with the project's values even before the collective spelled them out. If working together on formulating the values makes them more aware of that, all the better!

While the vision stays open to adjustments, the values never change, even if the source person transmits her source responsibility to a successor. Values constitute the permanent identity of the project, like a central thread throughout the currents of its history and across all the generations of people who will source it into the future. Values are the strongest expression of what the project is: change the values, and it becomes a different project.

Together, the vision and values constitute the soul of that first initiative, which we can imagine as the project's DNA—its essence in terms of identity and purpose (what and why). The vision and values set the project's framework, for which the source person is responsible. This is why it's not at all rare to see a source person (who may otherwise be quite consensus-oriented) forcefully intervene when her project's values are ignored or its vision thwarted. In fact, she's just carrying out, with all the required zest, her role as guardian in service to the project.

Now that we know the source person's three roles, we can wrap up the definition like this: the source person gets an idea or vision, takes initiatives and risks to make it happen, and determines what the next steps are to materialize the idea, always ensuring respect for the values and vision as she herself sees them.

Entrepreneur, guide, guardian: isn't that the same as being a responsible person? And where am I in relation to these three roles when I carry out my own responsibilities? Let's think about it for a few moments before we continue.

# Chapter 3

## *Recognizing yourself as source and living it out*

IN nature, a spring begins as a hidden water reservoir, dormant within the earth. A sudden change in the terrain—a fissure, or a shift—lets it spring out in a free flow. Something like that happens to the source person. He has a set of skills, a personality, a life history—the fertile ground from which, seemingly all at once, an idea emerges. Just as water goes its own way, the source person gets his *ergon* going, forming his own river bed across the landscape (taking initiatives and risks) and making detours (when doubts arise about the next step). Water flows freely and abundantly toward an ever-receding horizon. Same for the source person, who not only launches his project, but also keeps it going and makes it prosper... provided he stays aware of his role as source, aware of the responsibilities and opportunities associated with a source person, and that he acts—indeed that he *lives* according to that awareness.

What's the difference between an amateur and a pro? There's a venerable saying that the amateur knows what to do, but the professional knows what *not* to do. So in my role as source person I'm more often an amateur than a professional. Just knowing what to do is not enough to position me as a source; I also have to be aware of all the things not to do—the things Peter Koenig accurately (if somewhat severely), calls "source pathologies". If I don't fulfil my responsibility as a source person, if I do it poorly, or insufficiently, this failure will directly impact my initiative, function, relationship, project—and the damage will continue to be felt over the long term. Just as the source person can be the project's most powerful driver, its main stumbling block can also be… its source person.

So how do I become a "pro" at this? By first of all recognizing my shortcomings as a source person, and then by adopting the appropriate remedies. We'll look at some of the maladies that can afflict "patients" in the source world.

**1. The source denier: disregards the role of source.** Both in numbers of patients and in impact on human initiatives, the leading disease source persons suffer from is undeniably the failure to recognize the nature, and the extent, of their role as source. This epidemic ravages our businesses, our institutions, our initiatives of every stripe, not to mention the suffering and waste of energy and resources that could be avoided if the source person could clearly see himself as source.

Although everybody knows I'm the one in charge, the source denier pretends no one's in charge, slamming the brakes on my project, my team, or the organization I'm the source of. At the same time, everybody looks at me with their questioning glances, using their wits to get me to indicate what the next step is. If you've lived through this, you'll be aware of the dramatic collateral damage this attitude can cause. It's awful to think back on the years I spent pretending—especially to myself—that I was *not* the source of a certain public interest association; meanwhile our oversight committee both wasted time and frazzled nerves in a merciless feud. It had come to this because for too long they'd been without the guide's compass, the guardian's maintaining the limits, and the entrepreneur's risk taking. It was as if the association's aeroplane was flying without a pilot—or with a pilot who was usually asleep at the wheel.

But maybe I'm being too hard on myself. A person who finds himself in the trap of source denial may have taken his first initiative with plenty of enthusiasm (as I had), but for understandable reasons he's now lost some of his passion. And sometimes the source person just can't quite imagine himself having the ongoing responsibility for his initiative—he might not feel competent to lead it, or he didn't think his initial idea would unfold in ways that would keep him really busy.

How do you fix this failure to recognize yourself as source? When taking an initiative, I should be aware, as a source person, of what I'm precipitating right in the moment when I'm initiating it. In my case, the memory of past mistakes has proven useful and helps ensure I take my source role increasingly seriously when launching a new initiative.

On the other hand, if the source person is absent for a long time without recognizing the fact, the correction process will be longer and more tiresome: he'll have to do some fundamental work on what's blocking him. It could be a question of modifying a character trait (laziness, habitual self-doubt or lack of self-confidence, for example, are frequent obstacles). Or it could be a matter of reining in a limiting belief ("I am incompetent", "my ideas are not interesting", "others do this much better than I" are common stumbling blocks). He might need to face some fears (of failure, of risk taking, of the initiative's scope, or of what people will say). Sometimes it's his own projection that needs to be reclaimed ("source responsibility is a power game", "communicating the next step is manipulation", and so on). Every source person has his own inner obstacles; here too, humans can be very creative!

Sooner or later, anybody who takes a source initiative will have to confront his personal weaknesses, whatever they are. And remember that the act of taking responsibility as source is a formidable catalyst for making those very weaknesses materialize. Everyone encounters these obstacles, they're part of life, but we're also invited to face up to them—if not to eliminate them, at least to mitigate their effects. By dialoguing or training with others, you can facilitate this process of recognizing yourself as a source person and learning to act accordingly. By exchanging experiences and having others' support in confronting old patterns, you'll

deepen your grasp of source principles and integrate them more easily: remember, we're relationship beings—we're all in this together!

The truth is, the most powerful thing a source person can do for the success of his initiative is to engage in this inner struggle—which is actually an expression of deep self-respect and self-love that allows him to fully realize himself in this human, noble and creative activity of "sourcing", and to bring into being things that would never have existed without him.

**2. The tyrant: mistakes ego for source.** The second major pathology we encounter in source persons is overdoing the source person's role — trying to be all too much source. This source person starts believing he's the possessor of his initiative and its ramifications, rather than a repository for them. Peter Koenig goes so far as to say the source person should literally be a dictator, one who dictates the next steps as soon as they become apparent to him, but this is not done by lording it over others or tyrannically wounding and devastating them.

The disease of over-sourcing causes even more damage when the afflicted source person is also the legal owner of his initiative (organized as a company, for example) or is the principal source of funds for his project. This false belief that ego and source are the same makes it even easier for him to see the prerogatives of the source role not as responsibilities but as ego-inflators. In its primary psychological sense, "ego" refers to a person's self-representation and self-awareness—which are eminently healthy and even essential for the balance of the personality. But in this book, I use "ego" in the ordinary and pejorative sense of a "false self-representation", as in the expression "egomaniac". Paradoxically, a person who is "too much" of a source would, through his behaviour, be failing to fulfil his source responsibilities. Instead of serving his project (as a source person is bound to do), he puts his project at the service of his personal appetites and co-opts it for his own agenda.

We've all met people who manage their project with an authoritarian hand. Constantly putting themselves forward, they give free rein to their anger and sometimes to their violence. By trying to control everything and leaving very little space for their collaborators, they make the laws and then flagrantly break them at will. Under their motto, "Don't do as I do—do as I tell you!" they proclaim authentic-sounding source principles that are contradicted by their actions. Their illness makes them prefer their ego's noisy suggestions to their source's subtle inspirations.

Paradoxically, their tyrannical attitude hides a distinct lack of trust in their "sourceness" and its natural authority. The patient confuses his own weaknesses with what he imagines to be the source's, and believes he is properly compensating for them by replacing the deficient source with his own hard-driving ego. He ends up trying to fulfil his source role using the wrong motor: he installs his ego's gas-guzzling combustion engine in place of the unpretentious—but powerful—photovoltaic efficiency of his source… Hello smog alert! Possibly the most disheartening outcome is that his initiative, project, business, relationship, will never achieve the full potential that his initial source inspirations might have opened up for him.

How do we cure this destructive disease? Just as with the source-denier, our tyrant will have to do some serious work on his most disabling character traits—on his lack of confidence, mistaken premises, fears and the limiting beliefs he projects onto fulfilling his source responsibilities. Sometimes you just have to suffer so much discomfort in your project or relationship that it finally wakes you up to start the work of introspection. Source persons on this inward path who resolutely grasp their pilgrim's staff transform themselves, sometimes dramatically, into luminous beings and humble and strong sources; the attraction of their project, once again fed by its original spring, is a beautiful testimony to this.

Once the source person has crossed the ego desert in search of the source, he begins to know himself better and to address his shortcomings. It's an excellent attitude, and resonates with Philip Neri's prayer (16th century) "Lord, beware of *Philip*!" With a little smile the source person could productively translate this to "Source! you'd better beware of *me*."

There's a devious variant of "too much source" that turns up not only in the main source person's exercise of his role, but also in relation to specific-source roles. This condition could be called the *source-usurper's* disease. It's a person who is infected (often unconsciously) with the ambition of taking the source person's place. Worming his way into the source person's role, the usurper tries to take it over. Of course, the effort is doomed, since the project's source—as carried in the heart of the source person—can only be transmitted by the original source person himself, freely and without coercion. No one can take it away from him. There's the case of Steve Jobs, source of Apple, who was forced to leave the company for 11 years. The source person can be physically excluded from his own project, but *will always remain the source person*, unless and until he actively transfers this source to someone else. What the source-usurper doesn't understand is that source is inalienable—and that attempts to take it over are by definition futile. The usurper penetrates, sometimes quite subtly, the project's decision-making spheres, trying to get "power" by occupying positions of influence, making sure his voice is heard everywhere, and taking every opportunity to trumpet his claim to be the real source. He may also brazenly try to take over a specific-source's field that has not been entrusted to him by the project's source.

The usurper acts like it's all about him and his urge to force his will on the enterprise—we can see that he (like the tyrant above) suffers from the ego disease. But in his case, the pathology can only develop in the physical or mental absence of the source person—in other words, where the source person has ignored his own responsibility as source. This disregard, as with the source denier, leaves a "source gap" for the hijacker to sneak through. Indeed, if he thinks he can replace the source person, it's down to the fact that the real source is failing to fully occupy the position. (Good luck with that.) The safest protection against a source usurper—whose vain insurrectional attempts can create confusion and do great harm to the project—is for the authentic source person to rise up and reclaim his role with decisive action and a confident heart. As for the source usurper himself, instead of lurking around someone else's "source", he would do well to discover and focus on what he is authentically the source of.

**3. The slacker: pays no attention to the work of source.** The third typical source pathology concerns people who, while they do recognize themselves as sources, don't make the move to take action based on it. They neglect the source's main tasks: listening to one's intuitions, taking initiatives and risks, clarifying the next steps, and defending the integrity of the values and vision. With his sluggish engine, the slacker ensures that his initiative as a source person, his project, won't come close to achieving its full potential. And there's worse to come: over time, the project reverts to survival mode, and soon the enthusiastic contributors—the ones who initially provided the driving force—begin to drop out in search of more engaging challenges. Depending on how much energy is still left in the project, this can take a longer or shorter time but it will certainly end up with the death of the initiative—unless the source person manages to escape this paralysing lethargy in time.

Any source person, at any time in his "source career", can fall victim to the slacker disease. Anyone can be hit by a period of engine-idling or lack of motivation, but a timely response can ensure the weakness will be short-lived. Admittedly, some people face stubborn obstacles in applying themselves to the work of source, for reasons similar to those afflicting the source-denier and his disregard of source. Here too the same remedies, practised alone, in dialogue or in groups, are effective: work on character and limiting beliefs, on fears, and on projections. But there are also some complementary remedies:

- *Make up your mind to act as a source person.* Do it not as an external objective to be achieved, but as an internal intention* that you renew through regular repetition. Intention is like flipping a switch, an ignition motor that triggers the spark to get your initiative going.

- *Take a step back to set the vision and clarify the next steps.* Follow the Beatles and "Turn off your mind, relax and float downstream—this is not dying…" For my personal practice of this, I regularly conserve some energy and earmark my agenda, devoting enough time alone and in groups to reflecting *as source*. I let myself slow down and widen my horizon to the "source's eye view", from where I can see my greatest added value as a source person: that thing that no one else can do in my stead. During these intervals, I entrust the operational details to others so I can stay attentive to my role as source.

- *Take responsibility from the source, joyfully.* Etymologically, the person "responsible" is the person who carries the response in himself. This expression matches the role of source person: he carries the initial idea, the one his first initiative was the "response" to. Next, he proceeds, through his ongoing work of clarification, to "respond" to the nettlesome question of what the next step will be; and finally, as a source person, aptly "responds" to the whole project by communicating about its values and vision, the course it will follow, its collaborators, its implementation. So for instance, if the next step means taking a risk, then living his source responsibility means jumping right in; if the next step is to take a further initiative, let's get going; if it's a matter of firing somebody, do it right away; and even if the next step is to do nothing for the moment, lie down in the grass and relax!
  So why "joyfully"? Because it's much more graceful and enlivening to express the answer we carry within us with a joyful heart. It takes practice, but it's what makes the source person's *ergon* into art.

Let's conclude our overview of the ways source can be blocked and weakened. The systematic description of the main pathologies isn't meant to imply that each disease follows a precise, clearly delineated process—in fact, the three illnesses interact with each other, and mix spontaneously.

At times, don't we all act like source deniers or tyrants? And you're not the only one who slacks off sometimes!

To visualize the range of source positions, imagine a cursor along a straight line, where one end represents zero personal involvement (slacker disease) and the other end represents 100% ego (tyrant disease). Those who can't even see the cursor represent the source-denier disease. In this model the source person's return to health would mean placing the cursor midway between the two extremes of neglecting the work of source and the tyranny of overdoing it. This middle ground is the place of virtue, says Aristotle (Greek philosopher, 4th century BC—see his *Nicomachean Ethics*, 1107a). He explains the middle ground of virtue as being "a perfection, not an average". We should picture it as a summit between shortfall and excess, a ridgeline, so to speak, that you can walk along, careful not to slip down one slope or the other. To live along this crest, to scramble back up to it when we slip down, is a dynamic, ongoing task for every source person: in our actions, we are constantly being invited to realize virtue's golden mean.

Recognizing yourself as a source, and living accordingly by moving your inner cursor to the virtuous middle, releases considerable energy into everything you're the source of—your initiative, your project, your job or your relationship. This energy is something the source person first develops within himself, in the form of his passion for the project. This passion is contagious, which he'll realize as soon as others come to join his project, igniting it with their drive and enthusiasm. His passion also gives him a light touch when it comes to exercising the source principles: no longer overwhelmed by his responsibilities as a source person, he joyfully responds to the great privilege of being an artisan and creator.

Do you feel this passion, this energy, in your own initiative?

Part Two
# SHARING SOURCE

# Chapter 4

## *Sources—global and specific*

FIRST you welcome source within yourself, then you share it with others—it's just in the nature of things. It actually is rare for a source person to conduct an initiative completely on her own, without anyone else's support. As a source person, I usually need others to help me realize my idea and put my initiative into effect. As I welcome others into my project, what part, in terms of source, am I going to share with them—and what am I going to keep in my own hands? That's the big question, and we'll answer it in three steps. First of all, in this chapter we'll go more deeply into how source responsibility is apportioned in a project; then (chapter 5) we'll look at the source person's relationship with the project collective as a whole; and finally (chapter 6) we'll explore source persons' collaborations among themselves.

Peter Koenig explains that when someone welcomes an idea, intuition, or inspiration and begins taking an initiative and risks to achieve it, she's creating a *field*. At this moment of creating the field, she becomes a source person. This is the playing field, the situation where her initiative develops into a project, enterprise, home, function, relationship. The field has its own shape, and its own boundaries that derive from the vision and values the source person discerns in her initiative. The field is like a living cell—it can be extended or contracted at will by the source person, depending on the project environment's potential for development.

The source person who has created this field stays responsible for its development over the long term; we call her the *global source* to signify her responsibility for the field as a whole—both its spatial extent and its evolution over time. She's the global source not by being the field's owner (she may or may not be), but by being responsible. To be source is a service, not a proprietorship. A global source carries out this responsibility not least via the roles of entrepreneur, guide, and guardian.

To advance her initiative, the global source needs the support of other people who show up to offer help. These helpers arrive in different ways: attracted by the initiative's energy and the global source's passion, they may rush to join in, or following her intuition, the global source may take the initiative to offer them a role within her project.

In welcoming someone into the project, the global source offers them a place in her field: she designates a portion of the field that the new arrival may consider his *own* playing field, his own personal work space within the project's field. In accepting this designation, he becomes the *specific source* of that part of the field, and from then on this new person will hold the full source responsibility for that part—which he'll in turn carry out through the roles of entrepreneur, guide and guardian, always in line with the framework (the vision and values) that the global source has defined for the project. Because from the moment the global source transmits a part of her field to a specific source, this person too begins to receive source intuitions, ideas, and inspirations about this part of the field, along with the energy needed to realize them. With regard to the specific source's patch of the field, however, the global source now no longer receives those gifts! Here we see the remarkable "source economy" that fully respects both the gift bestowed by the global source and the fundamental role of the specific source. Besides ensuring much greater efficiency in implementing the project, this transfer of intuitions from one person to another underlines the fact that source, although invisible, is something substantial.

Although a single project can accommodate numerous specific sources in the course of its development, there is only one *global* source for each first initiative, each project, enterprise, opera, house or relationship. Even if a team has been there from the beginning, it's that one unique person who took the first initiative and the first risk. It sometimes takes several searches or interviews to find out who that person is, but it's worth the trouble because if it's not clear who the project's global source is, then that source person is obviously in trouble—infected by source-denial disease or slacker syndrome (chapter 3). Also, this lack of clarity about the project's source person leaves the field wide open for a source-usurper (infected by the tyrant's disease) to trample over the terrain.

Having been entrusted with a part of the playing field, a specific source can then bring someone else into his own portion. Functioning as a kind of global source in relation to them in that context, the specific source welcomes others to his part of the whole, always maintaining the role of specific source relative to the project as a whole. In the final analysis, *each person* who collaborates on the project must be able to consider him- or herself the specific source of a *part*, no matter how large or small, of the field, and to invest in it by taking initiatives and risks, all the while receiving intuitions and clarifications on the next steps.

This cascading dissemination of sources, global and specific, functions as a network resembling a river delta. It constitutes the principal wealth of a project, uniting the different parts of the field with each other. It ensures their continuity and cohesion by providing a communal reference to the same global source, it takes advantage of a watershed of ideas and intuitions coming from all over, and it parcels out appropriate responsibility among its members. In a project where sources are well distributed, each has his own role and can spread his own talents.

This cascade of sources reminds me of a company where I once worked. As the first Internet provider in Switzerland, it was founded by a then-unknown visionary, Pierre Hemmer. At a time when most people had no idea of what the Internet was, Pierre got the idea of making it

available to the public. As a great example of a global source, and realizing the enormity of his task, Pierre quickly brought collaborators, especially engineers, into his project, and deliberately entrusted them with portions of his field. Intuiting that the spread of the Internet was much more of a human and social matter than a technical one, he began to include experts in other fields: archaeologists, linguists, a philosopher, making them each a project manager. In the client interface, these culture specialists did a better job than the technicians. Pierre invited each new arrival to create his own job, to shape it by taking advantage of the freedoms of the emerging new web professions. Though of course the source vocabulary was still in the future, what he wanted was to make each one of us a specific source fully responsible for his own realm. He may have had some source maladies, but this hindsight takes nothing away from the immense credit he deserves for introducing his forty collaborators to the three source roles of entrepreneur, guide, and guardian. His vision caught on and spread: when the Internet bubble burst in 2001 and his company folded, his former collaborators promptly founded no less than seven new enterprises—including my own Ordinata—based on their unique experience: their training as specific sources gave them the courage and enthusiasm to launch their own initiatives as global sources. I owe this exceptional man my heartfelt gratitude for trusting me with various positions in the cascade, making my "source apprenticeship" possible.

A project's cascade of sources can be visually represented by a large circle (the global source's field) containing several different-sized circles (the playing fields of specific sources), some of which contain other smaller circles (specific source persons' specific sources). And each one of the circles corresponds to a source person. To better understand who's involved in a project, and how they're connected, you can map these source relationships using the Maptio software developed by Tom Nixon, one of the key players in Peter Koenig's network (www.maptio.com).

The resulting image of nested circles will show, at a glance, the totality of a project's source persons and the relationships among them. It reveals the natural order of collaboration at the heart of the project, and offers an interesting—and significantly distinct—complement to traditional organizational charts. These emphasize the "how", whereas the cascade of sources depicted by the nested circles sheds light on the "why". Instead of the familiar hierarchical relationships—with their infamous sluggishness and bias—the cascade of sources represented by nested circles reflects the organic links among the sources. In other words, it clarifies their complex relationships as people who can receive intuitions, take initiatives and risks, keep an eye on the task (the next step), share vision, values and ideas (the global source person's), and all the while enrich the project with their own vision, values and ideas (the specific source person's). These magnify and complement the global source's, so that the cascade of sources flows freely in every direction. Ultimately, the nested circles represent the total responsibility each person has for the extent and evolution of the field (or the part) entrusted to them.

These organic links among sources, illustrated here by images of the cascade and the reservoir, give rise to a form of "hierarchy" that offers new meaning to the word—which, as Peter Koenig reminds us, originally referred to a sacred order. The network of sources arises not at all by chance, but follows an implicit order where each person has her role to play and takes overall responsibility according to her own place in the project's field.

This "total" responsibility that each one takes—how can that possibly work? First we said that the global source person, once she's initiated the project, takes full responsibility for the totality of the field (space) and its development (time). But we also insisted that the specific source has total responsibility for *his* portion of the project field. These two responsibilities appear to overlap and could possibly interfere with each other: how to reconcile them?

Thinking along with Aristotle's notion of analogy, let's say *both* source persons are fully responsible, but not in the same way. It's all a question of perspective: instead of considering responsibility as an unequivocal notion with only one definition, let's consider it an analogical reality that can be understood in multiple ways, depending on the nature of the object and the angle of view we adopt when looking at it.

From the perspective of a specific source person, his responsibility for his part of the field is *total*, because it's up to him to fully inhabit the roles of entrepreneur, guide, and guardian, fulfilling all the source responsibilities that this implies: opening himself to receive intuitions, clarifying each next step, and taking risks—all things that the global source will not do for him. At the same time, from the standpoint of the global source, the specific source's responsibility is *relative*, because he's charged with ensuring that the vision and values of the project as a whole are respected and promoted in that part of the field he's responsible for. This means he has to reconcile the global source's "imposed" framework with his own vision for the future of his own portion. In addition, the specific source's responsibility is relative in the sense that he's received his mandate from someone else.

If we look at the global source's responsibility, we find a curiously similar situation: as a global source she has *total* responsibility for the project, and this of course includes the part the specific source is responsible for. To this is added her own responsibility for the framework (vision and values) that she recognizes as the project's.

From the perspective of the specific source, however, the global source's responsibility is also *relative*, since in order to exercise her responsibility for the totality of the project, she depends on the support of specific sources, who exercise theirs at the level of their part of the field. Another way the global source's responsibility is relative is that she's also called upon to hold the vision and values—the framework she herself has established.

These seemingly incompatible perspectives can be reconciled by considering that the global source and the specific source are each totally responsible in their own domains and at the same time mutually dependent upon each other. This paradox is something that ancient and mediaeval philosophers resolve through the concept of "reciprocal causality of total causes"*. Without detracting from the source responsibility of either one, this mutual dependence in fact connects them with each other's responsibility. The global source's concern is with the project as a whole, including the project's framework, while the specific source's is to an area within the project: both of them carry out these responsibilities by fully exercising—each in their designated field according to their position relative to the whole and their own dependence on the other person—the total responsibility of a source person: as entrepreneur, as guide, and as guardian. So whether I am a specific source or a global source, I am invited to fully live my source responsibility, knowing that it's interconnected with the responsibilities of the other sources.

Source responsibility can also be expressed in terms of power and authority. Peter Koenig invokes the distinction that coach Robert Hargrove makes between power (the ability to act) and authority (understood as the right to act). Philosopher Myriam Revault d'Allonnes* offers an illuminating perspective that sees power as referring to *space*, while authority has to do with *time*. Applying this view to the topic of source, a source person exercises her full power in the *space* of the field (or portion of it), and she exercises authority through the development of the field over *time*.

The idea of "power" can be problematic today, associated as it is with constraints, the use of force, giving out orders and punishments, imposing one's will, and controlling everything. With this understanding of power, we sense the predominance of an inflated ego—a source person who confuses her power in this way is in danger of contracting the tyrant's disease. In fact, the source person's power should be seen differently: it is rather the full ability and complete right to summon and gather the energy necessary to take care of her field (or her portion of it) and of its future.

The source person's *power* emerges at the same time as her field (or the part of it that's attributed to her) is born. By creating (or agreeing to care for) this field, she puts her initiative into the space of the field, and has the power to extend its dimensions at any time: both the area of it (always in line with the field's environment), and the depth of it (through uncovering the field's hidden treasures). Peter Koenig refers to these treasures when he says of the source person that "the field is extended by every conversation she has"—because each one widens her field of awareness. The source person's power lasts as long as the scope of the project exists (or that part of it that's been conferred on her). No one can exercise that power in her stead. Not a specific source trying to take over the source's power, as he would then be a source-usurper, nor any global source trying to neutralize the specific source's power, as this would mean revoking the latter's mandate.

Exercising the power of source is carried out over time through the source person's *authority*. The word itself comes from the Latin *augere*, meaning to increase. The source person's authority over her field or her portion of the field is meant to augment it, to make it evolve. Within the exercise of authority, psychologist Ariane Bilheran* identifies three main functions that are perfectly congruent with the source person's roles whether global or specific:

- a *generating* function, where authority creates *the origins*, the foundations. This corresponds to a source person taking an initiative in her role as entrepreneur, and particularly to the very first initiative taken by a global source;

- a *conserving* function, where authority underwrites the origins and protects their *identity*. This is consistent with the source person's role as a guardian ensuring that the vision and values are respected;

- a *differentiating* function, where authority makes it possible to evolve beyond the initiative's original identity to become a *project*, and in so doing, gives it a future. This connects with the source person's role as a guide making successive clarifications about the next steps in order to fuel the process of development, of ongoing evolution.

As we see, these ideas about authority and source line up with source principles: by fulfilling her roles as source, the source person exercises her authority over her project, function, business, team, house, etc.—which she brings into existence, conserves, and develops over time. And it's through her authority that she exercises her power, including her full ability and right to summon the energy to take care of her project. So authority is much more than a simple attribute of power: for the source person, it is the effective power.

This explains why for the source person force and coercion are unnecessary (they are instruments of the ego in its pejorative sense) to implement her vision or make people adhere to the next steps. If she communicates based on her source-authority, that in itself is enough for her collaborators to follow her, freely and unforced, because they will have grasped the meaning and relevance of her vision. This doesn't mean a source person never raises her voice: sometimes in order to wake up those who may have lost track of the project's field and framework, she has to clearly restate those parameters. It's not always easy, so let's keep an eye on the cursor described in chapter 3, and place it just in the middle between "too little engagement" and "too much ego".

In this chapter we've found that the source person has power over his or her project by exercising authority, and that it's through doing this in the roles of entrepreneur, guide, and guardian that his or her source responsibilities are fulfilled. We've seen how this responsibility is distributed and shared among specific sources and the global source, and how, in this situation of mutual dependence they are naturally led to collaborate—to coexist within the project collective. In the next chapter, we'll take a closer look at the way source and collective interact with each other.

But before you move on, ask yourself how, in your own collective, source responsibilities are being distributed.

# Chapter 5

## *The source develops the collective*

---

THROUGH the act of initiating a project, its global source brings the collective into existence. The project's collective is born at the moment the global source welcomes specific sources into his field to help achieve the initial intuition. That's where the interaction begins between source and collective. Just as in nature, where a single source emerges from the earth, and with its downhill flow, a watercourse appears. Tributaries arrive to reinforce it, forming a torrent and then a river. These additions join up with the watercourse because it's moving in a direction that suits them. When the contributing water molecules join the flow, they don't change: they just mix into water that's already streaming along. All together, the water begins its long voyage to the sea.

It's the same with our human projects and endeavours. The global source initiates the project's collective by inviting others to come in, offering them specific-source responsibilities that will help achieve the source person's vision in a way that respects his values. The specific sources join because it seems to them that the project will contribute to realizing their own visions, and that it corresponds to their own personal values.

In the end, this is why each source—global or specific—takes part in the project and therefore in *the collective*: because the tasks and purpose of the project (see "pathway" and "purpose" in chapter 2) align with that person's own vision and personal values. This is obviously true for the global source, since he's invested the initiative with his own values and vision, but it's just as true for a specific source, who recognizes an opportunity to express her own values—which resonate with those of the project—and to a certain extent to realize her own particular vision, while promoting the project's vision and values.

By the same token each source, according to the particular mission, contributes both to the project's unfolding and also, over time, to the collective's development. The specific source contributes by developing the part of the field she's responsible for—relying on, in addition to her intuition, the advice of her colleagues to clarify the next steps in the stages of this evolution, and wherever possible by promoting synergies with her colleagues' developmental initiatives. As for the global source, he develops the collective by attracting new recruits and also welcoming those who turn up spontaneously, inviting them all to become specific sources. He stimulates the synergies among them, dialogues with them in his process of clarifying the next steps, and, in order to reinforce the collective culture, periodically reminds them of the project's vision and values.

Note that the global source focuses on the single purpose of achieving his project, and concentrates most of his energy on this. For him the goal is not the collective *per se*. Rather, it's an indispensable means to achieving the project—and it's the *project* that motivates him to develop the collective.

When I started Ordinata in 2001, there were two of us—and for over a dozen years that's how it stayed. But in my original vision I'd imagined a larger team, or even several teams. When my associate decided to change course and I found myself on my own, I took a chance on forming a new collective around the vision and values of Ordinata. Once I clearly expressed my intention to myself, I was surprised to see how the candidates started flowing towards me. After a few years we grew into two teams—one French and one German speaking. Although I, as global source, did in fact create the two collectives, the specific sources actively contributed to this development by participating in the enhancement of our services, and by making improvements in the way we run our business, in particular through our regular in-house workshops.

Increasingly, global sources recognize "participatory dynamics" as an advantageous way of supporting the collective's development. This method of management and governance emerged from a successful collaboration between me (in Switzerland), Martine Marenne (in Belgium, www.dynamiqueparticipative.be), and our respective teams. Ordinata, like our Belgian partners, actively supports many collectives and trains a considerable number of people, seeing them through the process of acquiring this innovative practice. With participatory dynamics (*dynamique participative*) we've revealed an art rather than a science, one aimed at encouraging and achieving the emergence of collective intelligence, collaboration, and synergy—not just at the collective's core, but also between the collective and its environment. The art of participatory dynamics deploys a number of concrete tools and methods, but particularly relies on soft skills. In fact, what we are cultivating here is the art of *"we"*. It's an approach that encourages integration among collaborators, enhances their adherence to the project's direction, stimulates innovation, increases the flexibility and relevance of their actions, makes the collective more agile, develops synergy among its members and reinforces their alignment with the vision and values of the project. With participatory dynamics, each member of the collective can express their views about what is vital to them and to the group, and can propose improvements: this is collective intelligence in action. The participatory dynamics method sets a high standard, which besides increasing know-how, aims to cultivate each member's interpersonal abilities.

Collectives that have introduced participatory dynamics employ it as a common language that everyone can use to express themselves and generate action together. If a collective entity adopts these dynamics, it's because they correspond to the source person's vision and values. Frédéric

Laloux's book, *Reinventing Organizations* has inspired many leaders in their search for new forms of management. In it he interviews various community and company founders, each of whom is the global source of his own initiative. These trailblazers are replacing traditional organizational hierarchy with more participative governance simply because the new forms correspond to their vision and values. Remove the global source from these initiatives, and the participative dimension they introduced loses its basis and its legitimacy. Just as he generates the collective, the global source creates the collective's participatory dynamics. Only then does the method become a shared concern among all the collective's sources. These are the people who will gradually introduce it into their teams. Together, global and specific sources share their source responsibilities through sharing responsibility for the collective.

Let's take an example of this shared responsibility between sources. A client of ours had a children's services organization in which several independent entities were grouped into a large foundation of about 150 collaborators. The global source of this new group intuited that introducing participatory dynamics could help get around the idiosyncrasies of the various discrete bodies and achieve unity as a single organization. After training himself in the process, he started to train his closest specific sources, the sector managers. As they in turn began to sensitize their teams to this new language, they experimented with the new decision-making and problem-solving processes. At the same time, the global source set up a kind of "strategic college" where about 30 employees and

managers had the opportunity to periodically contemplate the big issues and make strategic decisions together about the collective's future. Some years later, to extend the scope of collective intelligence and shake up the hierarchy, the eight top managers invited seven employees (one from each sector) to join them on the management team, on those occasions when there were important operational decisions to be made. Now, the strategic college and the management team replace their employee-members every three years with new ones, so that eventually all the specific sources will have an opportunity to participate in the foundation's management. Along with this, of course, is the ongoing experience they gather of working with participatory dynamics in their own teams. Little by little, participatory dynamics becomes a common language the collective's sources can use to align with each other as they advance toward realizing the project's vision.

Participatory dynamics offers a way to help source persons, wherever they're situated in the project's field, to dispel their doubts about the next step in the area they're responsible for. By formulating questions, objections and proposals, especially in the core process of decision by consent, the contributions of the other collective members can be decisive for a source person trying to clarify the next step. This process is a concrete and very effective implementation of the dialogue outlined in chapter 2.

Once a collective has adopted participatory dynamics, two principles govern the way it works: *equivalency* and *primacy*. They especially demonstrate the source person's importance in promoting and guaranteeing participatory management and taking care of the collective.

- The principle of *equivalency* recognizes that each of the players has an equal value and has the same ability to influence the collective's vital decisions. This principle establishes the fundamental equivalence among all human beings, whether they are specific sources or global sources—or even if they aren't yet even conscious of what they're the source of: each one of them can become a source, and a force for bringing forward proposals. This is what's behind the participatory dynamics practice of holding decision-making meetings in a circle. The arrangement symbolizes equivalency by placing each participant equidistant from the centre, where the proposals to be decided upon are held.

- The principle of *primacy* recognizes that due to his power and authority regarding the project and his special responsibility for its vision and values, the global source protects the emergence, identity and development of the project, and consequently of the collective itself. His primacy consists in the group's—and his own—recognition of his unique role in service to the project. In participatory dynamics, this recognition doesn't mean he's entitled to capriciously lay down the law. Rather, it means he can give the benefit of his insights to the collective, can indicate the direction of the project's vision, can ensure that its values and framework are respected, and can make his authoritative voice heard through his encouragement, his objections, and through expressing the clarity he's acquired about the next step.

Over the course of arriving at a decision by consent, the global source receives the support of specific sources to achieve clarification on the next step: the decision-making process continues until the next step is completely clarified, which ultimately happens (in conformity with the principle of equivalency) thanks to questions, objections and proposals from specific sources. No decision is made until the global source is 100% clear about which step to take next. At that point it's enough to communicate his clarity to the others—they will freely consent, instinctively respecting the primacy principle: even if some of them still harbour doubts, they have confidence in the global source. So the global source's *clarity* is the determining factor for the success of a decision by consent, while the main means for the collective to arrive at this clarity comes from the specific sources' contributions during the process. The principles of equivalency and primacy complement each other to enable the collective to reach a perfect balance between the responsibilities of the various sources, global and specific. Remove *equivalency* and the collective falls back into an unmotivated old-school hierarchy; remove *primacy* and the collective is enfeebled, unable to make decisions. Having lost awareness of the global source's essential role, the collective becomes disconnected from the source's clarity and can no longer benefit from his work as entrepreneur, guide and guardian. Participatory dynamics gives a voice to each source in the ensemble of the collective, and is based on the simultaneous, linked exercising of the two principles. Without it, the art of "we" is dead in the water.

How do equivalency and primacy play out in your collective? To further develop your project's collective, what could you initiate?

Before going any further, a few words need to be said about a widespread form of collective that is nevertheless quite mysterious: the couple. As Peter Koenig points out, the relationship of those who live in twos doesn't escape the role distribution between a global and a specific source. One of them is the source of the relationship, having taken the initiative and the first risk. The other one, having accepted the invitation to enter into a relationship, has joined the project. That makes one of them the global source, and the other one the specific source, of their relationship. It's important for them to know which is which, so they can work out where each one's responsibilities lie. In philosophical terms, I would say that the two persons share the same relationship: the global source by being its *principle*, or starting point, and the specific source by being the relationship's *term*, or destination. It's like a train line that has a starting station and a terminal: the train itself continually passes back and forth from one to the other, and that's what happens in a couple.

To be the global source in a relationship is neither better, nor does it confer more status, than being a specific source. For the former it's simply a question of maintaining a certain vigilance about the development of the relationship *as such*, with regard to clarifying the next steps of the relationship's evolution over time. For the other one, it's a matter of contributing to that very evolution by developing, within the relationship's field, those parts he or she has accepted responsibility for. Because each couple is different, it's difficult to give examples that apply to everybody. For some specific sources, this area of responsibility might be initiating exchanges, sourcing shared activities, or opening up topics of conversation that further the relationship. The good brought by the specific source into the relationship is often decisive, especially when the global source is suffering from one of the source pathologies mentioned earlier. For a relationship to prosper, it helps if there are two people involved!

Yet the specific source in a relationship may also be the global source of various aspects of their communal life: that person could be the source of the living space, for example, of financial stability or home repairs, of common activities such as the next holiday destination or Saturday jogging, of gardening or shopping, of the couple's spiritual renewal, or maybe the source of planning the arrival of a child. Wherever one or the other takes an initiative as well as a risk, that person automatically becomes the global source and invites the other person to accept the role of specific source.

In your couple, how are global and specific source roles shared out? It can be very interesting to discuss the unique ways you distribute sources between you—being mindful about this helps develop synergies in your collective-for-two. And it's a great place to practise your source skills.

# Chapter 6

## *Seeing the source in each person*

IN the preceding chapters we've seen how the global source and the specific sources share source responsibilities without diminishing them, and how both types of source persons develop the collective, working together to implement their common project. To round out this portrait of shared responsibility among sources, in this chapter we'll explore how source persons collaborate within the project, particularly from the standpoint of their fundamental—and indispensable—attitude of mutual recognition.

To recognize source in the other appears to be the key to maintaining fruitful relationships among source persons—by which I mean relationships that are not only nourishing for the people concerned, but that are simultaneously, and fully, at the service of achieving the common project.

In addressing the "source denial" malady (chapter 3), we're now aware of how important it is, both for the source person and her initiative, that she recognizes *herself* as source. Now, we'll learn that it's just as vital for her to recognize source in *others*.

First of all, let's admit that to publicly recognize oneself as the source of an initiative can be daunting. You could, for instance, be afraid of how other people will see you, afraid to make a spectacle of yourself, to look like you're promoting yourself. But when you overcome your misgivings and openly acknowledge being the source of a project, your fellow collaborators will quite naturally recognize it and mobilize to help you achieve it. Here comes the energy: it's the first consequence of recognition.

It could happen that a person just can't, or won't, recognize source in another—the extreme version of this attitude is the source-usurper described earlier (chapter 3), but this nonrecognition can also appear in a multitude of more subtle forms: not recognizing the originator of an idea that I've appropriated, or failing to mention the genesis of an insight I've presented as my own, or using software without paying the license fee. But as Peter Koenig explains, failure to acknowledge source will boomerang back at me, sapping the energy of my initiative—the very project for which I tried to steal a bit of source from someone else. In the end, I won't profit much from my crime. In addition, the "thief" isn't the only one to suffer—my attitude will have negative repercussions for everyone, but especially for the source person I've stolen from, the person I've committed an injustice against. It's clear that organizations experience innumerable conflicts and suffer widespread injury as a result of "stealing source". Having said that, let's recall that in actual fact it's impossible to steal source from someone: the role of source is inalienable. If you're the initiator of something, you're its source, period. All the denial in the world won't change that.

This very book is a concrete example of the correlation between recognition and energy. If I had written it without referring explicitly to Peter Koenig as the "founding father" of source principles, not only would this injustice against him constitute plagiarism, it would have done me no good at all. My readers, for example, might have felt that something was not right about the message, this unease could make it harder for them to grasp the actual source principles, which would negatively impact both the principles' diffusion and some readers' motivation to follow up with group training or individual coaching with a specialist. It was obvious to me that a book about source would have to acknowledge the person who developed the source vocabulary and was the first person to research the principles, so I offered Peter Koenig "the last word" which he accepted by writing the afterword. The energy that recognition of source has given my project, even before the book saw the light of day, has been phenomenal, believe me: it has greatly facilitated the writing process, with my thoughts quickly organizing themselves and the words flowing like magic. Ever since I began to write it, my own efforts to further the spread of source principles have been carried along by Peter Koenig's own energy.

One more curious paradox: at first glance, it can seem like acknowledging another's tune could risk diminishing and dulling my own. But in reality it's the other way round: my acknowledgement amplifies and embellishes my own song. Together, our songs can become a chorus.

What are some other ways a global source can acknowledge source in others? First of all, the global source makes sure that the mandates she gives to those on her playing field are really specific-source mandates. That means they clearly come with the power and authority to take real responsibility for their part of the field. Although empowering and authorizing someone is a developing process that doesn't suddenly happen overnight, it's essential that the global source acknowledge the specific source as such—otherwise how will his colleagues and collaborators recognize him?

The global source of a project creates another significant form of acknowledgement when she recognizes the specific source as being the *global source* of an initiative *within* the project. For example, Evelyn, a junior assistant in a governmental education department, has an intuition about a better way to classify the copious files circulating around and around throughout the department, and her system would better serve her colleagues' needs. When she presents her idea to Marc, the global source of the department, he promptly approves it, having seen that her idea fits perfectly with his vision of developing the department and implementing its values of efficiency and collaboration. So Marc appoints Evelyn to carry out her classification proposal, and he informs her

co-workers about the project, asking them to refer any questions or problems about it directly to her. By doing this he acknowledges, in front of everyone, Evelyn's power and authority in this project.

At that point, Marc could stop. Instead, he decides to take it a step farther, since he wants both to support Evelyn in her classification project and to emphasize that he recognizes her as a global source: he tells her that she can count on his help if needed. In other words, he proposes *himself* as a specific source of the project that Evelyn is global source of.

Evelyn's initiative is an example of developing a project within the field of the department's global source (Marc's field). It can happen, as Peter Koenig explains, that a specific source's initiative considers launching a project outside the global source's field. Imagine for a moment that Evelyn is so strongly motivated by her experience of innovating in the field of filing that she gets the idea of proposing the improved activity to other departments that are actually outside of Marc's global field. By embracing a project which Evelyn is clearly the global source of, Marc has put himself at her service as a specific source (and shows it by promoting this new activity to his fellow department heads). But Evelyn's project has also extended Marc's global field, which now includes a nationwide archiving service. Many company expansions work like this.

This practice of "switching hats", where a specific source becomes a global source or vice versa, helps collaboration among members of a collective to flow that much more smoothly. Anyone can put himself at the service of another's project. Simply recognizing the other's role as source person brings a surge of energy—not only in one's own activity, but in the other's too. And this is where the boundary—sometimes considered too strict a line, but thoroughly pertinent and necessary—between the specific source's role and that of the global source can be eased: at any one time, a person can find himself to be a specific source and at another time, a global source. The more agile we become in moving flexibly from one role to the other, the more successfully we'll achieve the synergies we need to accomplish our projects.

Up until now this analysis has focused on the global source's recognition of a specific source, but it works the same way with the recognition that two specific sources give each other, either as a specific source in charge of a portion of the field, or as the global source of a particular initiative within it. Their attitude of respect, goodwill and sincerity is embodied by their acknowledgement of the other person's responsibility. This can only benefit their relationship, which in turn will reflect positively on their common project.

Speaking of relationships, let's remember Peter Koenig's observations (chapter 5) that in any relationship between two people there is a global source: it's the person who took the initiative and took the first risk. Over time, new initiatives may make way for global and specific source roles to be passed back and forth between these two people, since they are each, in turn, a global or a specific source of projects that spring from the ground of their relationship. Recognizing the other's source role, but also one's own, makes it clear who's responsible for what, which makes life steadier and more congenial. Some time ago, one of my sons complained about how he was always the one who had to take the initiative to set up the next meeting with his friend. It was getting to be tiresome, so he toyed with the idea of not reaching out for a while, just to see what would happen. But on reflection (spurred by Dad...) he realized that he was simply the global source of this friendship, and that the "next steps" (including their next meeting) were therefore up to him. And his friend had implicitly recognized my son's global source role. By leaving the initiative to my son, his friend had tacitly demonstrated his logical recognition of my son's global source role. Noticing this helped my son come to terms with his responsibility in the relationship.

As we've seen, collaboration among sources in the same project, enterprise, team or relationship is strengthened by their mutual recognition. However, this collaboration is not an end in itself. Sometimes it's not possible, or even desirable, to pursue it, and when that happens it should be acknowledged. When a specific source goes outside of the project's vision, or disrespects its values, the global source should intervene: that's part of her role as guardian. If the incompatibility looks to be permanent, the global source withdraws the mandate from that specific source, and asks him to leave the project. On the other hand, if a specific source becomes convinced that the evolution of the project he's participating in won't permit him to develop his own vision and personal values, he should face the consequences and leave the project to join (or create!) one that is a better fit with his personal aspirations. In either case, fully recognizing the way it is will allow the project, as well as the person leaving it, the opportunity to recover the energy and momentum to move forward. In fact, when someone leaves the field for good reasons and there's mutual understanding of this, there can even be a celebration, not only of all the things they've achieved together within the project, but also of the advancement of the leaving person's source.

Another significant aspect of recognition is the acknowledgement that the source, global or specific, gives to his project's collective. As Martine Marenne says about source principles, "a source owes it to her collective to honour the gifts they give her. That way the source communicates to people working on the project how important it is that they're there." In other words, the source must keep in mind that without the collective "we", her project wouldn't be where it is. It's not just a question of recognizing the contribution of everybody who works together in the project field to realize its vision and values, but also of bearing witness to the support the project's sources get, as guides, from the collective. Every source who turns to the collective can, by dialoguing with the others, receive valuable help in clarifying the next step. This help isn't just the individual contribution that each participant may offer separately, but is also the fruit of their communal reflection: the resonance among individuals has generated collective intelligence. The collective is acting as an incubator, the fertile ground from which the clarity emerges. But here we note Peter

Koenig's warning never to make collective intelligence into an entity with an independent existence. Rather, collective intelligence is a dynamic reality that emerges from simultaneous exchanges among members of the collective, and must be continually recreated anew. When each member of the collective reflects and acts on the basis of his or her own source, the collective intelligence bubbles up and becomes synergy. In receiving that kind of support from the collective, my attitude is more of *welcoming* than of *taking*—because a source, global or specific, does not egotistically help herself to the collective as if it were an "all you can eat" restaurant. Instead, she's at the service of the project, in collaboration with the other collective members. What keeps each one motivated to contribute is really this attitude of welcoming the offerings of the others.

All this should be convincing enough: there has to be mutual recognition among all the project sources if we want to achieve effective cooperation in our collectives. We've seen its significant effects: recognition makes more energy available for projects and people, and promotes synergy and working together among stakeholders. It strengthens relationships between people and clarifies questions of territory; in both area and depth, it can even extend the scope of the source field. Acknowledging source is so important for the development of projects, individuals and the collective, that at Ordinata most of the partners' "source-evolution" interviews (which replaced the outdated "annual evaluation" interviews) are devoted to it. So we ask questions like, in this company, what are you source of? What do you want to become source of? How can you develop your source? How can you help others develop theirs? The insights and reciprocal recognition expressed in the course of these interviews increase our personal motivation and our desire for collaboration. Needless to say, we find again and again that these encounters leave us in buoyant spirits.

What challenges associated with recognizing source have you encountered in your business or project? What source could you acknowledge more explicitly in your co-worker or teammate? How about in your spouse?

**Part Three**
# TRANSMITTING SOURCE

# Chapter 7

## *When the time is ripe, pass it on*

ECCLESIASTES, a collection of wisdom embedded in the Hebrew Bible, wants us to remember that "to every thing there is a season, and a time to every purpose under heaven" (Ec 3, 1). I recalled those words when Martine Marenne, the Belgian global source of the "participatory dynamics" methodology, explained the source person's three main progressions: "There's a time to receive, and a time to transform what you've received; and there's a time to pass it on". Up to now we've explored the way the source first receives, and then implements what she has been given. We've now come to this third and last "season", that of transmission. We'll go into three aspects of it—what it means, how it works, and how it's communicated. In this chapter we'll look at what it means to transmit source. Then we'll consider how to enact the transmittal (chapter 8), and finally we'll discover the challenges of disseminating source principles in our own environments (chapter 9).

A source can be transmitted horizontally or vertically. Horizontal transmission would be when a global source turns over a portion of his project field to a specific source (chapter 4), or when that specific source transfers her piece, or part of it, to another specific source. Vertical transmission is a more radical move: it happens when the global source of a whole project, initiative, item of real estate, or relationship relinquishes it to another person. Any transmission of source, whether it is horizontal or vertical, is brought about individually, from one person to another. It's actually impossible to transmit source to an organization or a group of people, because source is an entirely *personal* responsibility—hence, it can only be passed on to *a specific person* in the group.

Before we tackle these two axes of transmission, let's take a moment to look at a few instances of the act itself, a strikingly dynamic, creative and meaningful process that occurs between two people. It's as if at a certain moment a source person passes the baton to someone else—who receives its inherent power, authority and responsibility, and can then continue on course accordingly. Playing sports is full of such meaningful receptions. Nathalie Sarthou-Lajus*, a philosopher who thinks about transmission and how it's enacted in human life, tells how she grew up in an intensely rugby-loving family that spent every Sunday together, gleefully immersed in meticulously analysing the fine points of passing the ball. In this fast-moving contact sport, the ball is passed to the receiver in game-changing moves. For the ball to be successfully transmitted, the passer holds it firmly and almost tenderly as the receiver—who must be perfectly available—comes within range. In a well-judged, split-second choice of the right moment, the passer slips the egg-shaped ball over to the receiver, who cradles it "as a precious treasure, unpredictable as an infant coming out of the mother's womb" (*Le geste de transmettre* 48).

The title of Nathalie Sarthou-Lajus' book translates as "enacting transmission". To help us see how transmitting the source is akin to passing life on, let's unpack this phrase, which parallels giving birth: a mixture of preparation and improvisation, dedication and letting go, where the conscious and unconscious are intermingled, in both the donor and the recipient. The actual transmission of source becomes possible when both parties possess enough freedom, trust, and willingness to take risks. Transmitting source has to occur in complete freedom: the global source needs the liberty to pass the source *to whomever he wishes*, and the new source should feel free to accept it or not. Not only that, the global source is free to transmit the source *whenever he wants to*—no one else, not even his successor, can determine his agenda. These twin freedoms—whomever and whenever—imply a guarantee that for the act of transmission to take place, the source person has to trust that his successor will embody source by appropriately exercising the roles of entrepreneur, guide and guardian outlined above. Without this trust, there can be no transmission. Seen from the receiving end of the handover, the person chosen to receive the source (the heart of the initiative) needs to trust the global source and his project, but must also trust her own capacity to meet the challenge of source responsibility. Each of them has to believe in the other and in himself or herself, at least enough to accomplish, together, the act of transmission. As with the couple-collective introduced earlier (chapter 5), in the process of handing over the baton one of them will be the *principle*, or starting point, and the other, *term* or destination of the source transmission. This is one single act, freely entered into by two people, that arises out of the relationship of trust that binds them together.

But watch out: trust is a conviction, not a certainty. By definition, it's accorded not after the fact, but prior to being a 100% sure that the other really deserves it—that's why it's called trust! The act of transmitting necessarily involves a risk, shared by both the donor and the recipient: neither one of them knows with absolute certainty whether the transmission will actually work out. Since from the beginning, risk taking is such an integral part of every source's role as entrepreneur, it's not surprising to also find it in the process of transmitting source. For each of the source persons, what does this risk add up to?

For the donor, the main risk is that the transmission will fail, and that the whole process will have to be started again. This is compounded by the fear of annihilation, of losing everything including oneself: what will become of me—in other people's eyes as well as in my own—when I'm no longer global source? In fact, according to Nathalie Sarthou-Lajus, for the one who's giving source away, "transmission has an element of tragedy, because it requires a sacrifice from the donor, and an act of

self-obliteration" (70). She explains that "the moment of transmission is a deeply relational and life-changing experience you can only have by consenting to a form of self-abandonment" (72).

For the one who's receiving source, the main risk is wasting time and energy—and also hurting her reputation if the transmission doesn't materialize. If that happens, she could take it as evidence that her fear of failure was justified, and that she's not up to the task. Even when transmission is successful, the receiver may discover a few skeletons in the closet—that is, besides its positive features, some of the project's negative aspects may have been passed on to her as well. For her, the main challenge will be creating something new out of the old, and keeping what is essential to the project while letting it evolve: it's the risk of being free while being true. Sarthou-Lajus sees that "transmission is a paradox. It calls for something like 'leaning in' to a tradition you didn't choose, in order to free yourself from its strictures by making it your own. Without freedom, tradition can be crushing. Without tradition, freedom just spins its wheels" (101). For Sarthou-Lajus, "to be a successor doesn't mean you take at face value what has been said and given to you, but that you question it and reinvent the heritage" (104).

Let's consider more closely how source transmission proceeds along each of the two axes, horizontal and vertical. Each time a global source confers a part of the project field on a specific source, he's engaging in a transmission that's *horizontal* relative to the surface of the global field. It must be *total* (the part is wholly given over to the other), but not necessarily *permanent*: the global source may recall the portion at any time, revoking the specific source's mandate. Ultimately it's more a question of delegating source than of transmitting it in the narrow sense. It's what happens every time we change service providers, such as accountancy services, IT, consulting, suppliers, maintenance—anyone at all who plays a role involving a certain scope of initiative within our project field. Similarly, internally revoking specific source mandates and conferring new source mandates are significant horizontal transmission steps for reengineering structures and redesigning tasks and responsibilities within an organization. Of course, in any horizontal reorganization, the global source will be concerned to proceed carefully and with respect for the people involved.

The other frequently encountered form of horizontal transmission is when a specific source transfers her part of the field—the part that's been conferred on her by the global source—to another specific source. While it's true that this kind of direct transmission between specific sources must happen with the blessing of the global source, it will only succeed when the specific source person who passes it on, as well as the person who receives it, both show they've fulfilled the key conditions of transmission: freedom-in-fidelity, trust-with-no-guarantee, and risk taking. At that point, the specific source's baton can be securely passed on.

Some time ago, an associate of Ordinata came to see me: she wanted to confer an important part of her activities to someone else, in order to be more available for tasks that motivated her more, and which therefore would be more valuable to the company. Basically, she wanted to revamp her portion of Ordinata's field, and already had an eye on someone we could engage to take her place, under her supervision, to carry out the activities she wanted to let go of. Needless to say, as the global source of the organization I was enthusiastic about her responsible taking of source initiative, so I hastened to give her my support. A short time later, there we were: Ordinata had one more on its team.

Sometimes when a specific source departs, the global source doesn't want to make a horizontal transfer, but prefers to take advantage of the temporary vacuum to redesign the topography of his project field and to consider the possibility of redistributing the responsibilities. The global source may take back the part of the field left by the departing specific source, and temporarily occupy it himself before entrusting it to someone else. This happened to a friend of mine who directs a managed care institution for seniors. He temporarily took over in the interim period after his infrastructure manager left, which made him his own specific source in this area. Once he got a good overview of this part of his institution's field, he redefined its contours and was able to entrust this specific source to someone else.

Let's move on to *vertical transmission*, where we enter the realm of "all or nothing". In a successful transfer, the global source transmits the entire source to his successor. He gives over the complete project—the whole field, including all the parts entrusted to specific sources: the soul of the project, its DNA, its achievements, its history, the important issues as well as every single detail. The global source entrusts the receiver not only with the project as it now stands, but also with its future. If the donor holds back even one portion, he in fact transmits nothing at all, because the global source's field is one, and is indivisible.

Vertical transmission of source is by no means a question of transferring shares. Martine Deschamps* explains that "passing it on is neither legal nor financial, but transmits intangible creative energy". She warns that even if you have "the best possible plan for transferring knowledge, power and shareholder ownership, and develop the best fiscal, financial and legal strategies in the world, it can still happen that you've completely failed to actually transfer your company!" (*Planifier sa retraite ou sa relève* 103, meaning "Planning your retirement or legacy"). This is exactly what happened to one of our clients—a big company that had bought a medium-sized SME and allowed its founder and global source to keep his position as the acquired entity's director. Instead of accepting a specific-source role within the global field of the acquired enterprise, this founder had sold off the whole company, but did not relinquish his role as global source of it. A few years of favourable economic conditions followed, and no one suspected anything. But when things got rough, it emerged that the global source of the acquired entity had in fact been pursuing his own project, which lay outside the scope of the enterprise as a whole, and was putting his own vision and his own values ahead of implementing those of the actual global source of the whole. Such a confused mess can't go on indefinitely. If the acquired entity's director does not agree to transfer his global source role to the head of the whole company, then that head will have to get rid of the so-called partner and his entity. At the end of the day, the global source will have to admit that, except on paper, this SME has never really been part of his field, nor has it been of any real use to the company.

Situations where global source was not transmitted are much more common than you might expect. A pass can fail for various reasons. In the messy case above, it was ignorance of source principles at the moment of selling the SME that allowed its founder to surreptitiously hang onto the global source role, which by rights he should have relinquished. Or a global source might decide not to pass it on, and so to let his project die when he leaves: that would be a matter of voluntary non-transmission. Then again, as sadly happens all too often, the global source's good intentions of attending to his legacy can be interrupted by death or a long absence. At that moment, his project has become sort of a "source-orphan". To demonstrate what's going on with this non-transmission, Peter Koenig evokes the image of *a torch falling to the groun*d when the global source disappears. It just lies there, but it's still smoking. Anyone can pick it up and rekindle the flame—becoming, in that moment, the new source of the project. This happened to our accountant after the unexpected death of her office's founder: she resolutely picked up the torch and continued her former boss's work. It also happens that the global source is no longer interested in his project and drops the torch, with or without a transmission attempt. If however the global source has dropped the torch and it's picked up by someone who has different values to the founder, this is tantamount to founding a new project on the assets of the old one and represents a significant cultural change. Finally, non-transmission of source can be due to not finding the right candidate. There's an association I founded, whose global source role I've been trying to transmit for several years now… often the main thing a global source needs is patience! And, of course, he must not forget that until he transmits the source, or decides to end the project, he doesn't stop being responsible for it in its entirety.

What happens to a project when the global source disappears without transmitting source? An initiative can plod along for a relatively long time using the available energy of the people involved, but the inexorable process of decline is already underway, showing up as loss of vitality, a sense of disorientation, lack of motivation, decreased activity, loss of meaning, dissolution of the collective, death throes, and finally the pre-programmed last gasp of the project—unless someone comes forward to pick up the disabled torch spluttering on the ground. The project is no longer able to benefit from the source person's intuitions, there is no longer anyone who feels responsible for clarifying the next steps in the project's development, no new initiatives are put forward, and all potential risks are avoided. In addition, where the transmission of source has been inadequate, the participatory dynamics are always in danger because the global source is no longer there to remind the collective of why they adopted that system of governance in the first place.

Of course, gentle reader, none of this will happen to you. As a source person reading this book, you are forewarned and forearmed with the awareness that transmitting source is a source responsibility, and you are firmly resolved to pass it on when the time is right. Aren't you?

The question remains of when to set the transmission in motion. Only the global source can rely on his source-intuition to sniff out the right moment. Dialogue with the successor, and reflection within himself, will help dispel his doubts about this—it's the next, and last, step he'll have to decide on for his project. And when the time is right for him, and the other feels equally ready, and when the conditions of mutual freedom, trust, and risk taking have all been fulfilled—only then can the hand-off be completed. In the next chapter, we'll find out how.

# Chapter 8

## *Transmitting source, step-by-step*

As we've seen in the previous chapter, transmitting source is an art prepared for and practised—an event as precious and incalculable as the pivotal moment of a rugby pass, or of a baby being born. Nathalie Sarthou-Lajus's evocative comparisons (chapter 7) helped us to delve into the ways which, when the time comes to pass along the source to someone else, an "enactment of transmission" takes place in our projects.

There are people who take this art very seriously and start planning far in advance of a transition. One is a client of ours, an executive director who some time ago (five years ahead of his expected retirement date) set up a schedule of everything he planned to do, as global source, to prepare the transmission. Even though it's still too early to definitively choose his successor (because the "next step" remains in the future), he's already schooling his collective in the participatory dynamics that will allow his eventual successor to take the reins under the best possible collaborative conditions. Meanwhile he's gradually preparing himself by practising the humility and letting go he'll need on the day of transmission.

By now you know that source transmission is anticipated far enough in advance to allow the transmitting source person to dispel her various doubts. She does this by clarifying the successive next steps of this crucial path meant to ensure her project's sustainability. She prepares for it using three ways of achieving clarity: listening to her intuition, taking stock of herself in dedicated moments of self-reflection, and dialoguing with other people (chapter 2). I regularly engage in such dialogues with people who are preparing to hand over global source—and it's something I love to do. I find it brings together the plan of the person herself with that of the project or enterprise; it's a wholehearted process where humility brushes up against grandeur, passion accompanies responsibility, and legitimate self-interest is balanced by generosity.

So yes, you should be prepared for this event. But concretely, how is source handed over? In fact, the "how" of transmission emerges from a broad spectrum of possible approaches that range from quite formal to very informal. No matter which transfer modality you choose, the moment of transmission will be with you, whether donor or receiver, as a stored memory for the rest of your life—and often this is also true for anybody lucky enough to be present at the handover! Once I witnessed a very formal—and utterly joyful—transmission between the director of a group care home and his successor. The two were surrounded by their co-workers and care beneficiaries, all of them gathered together and deeply touched to be there for the event. At the culmination of the day-long transmittal, they each spoke; then the director handed over a symbolic object to the person who would be replacing him. It was clear to all that the global source had been transmitted.

There are definite advantages to a formal transmission: it nicely distinguishes before from after, and delineates the one in charge from the one no longer in charge. In a formal transmission, the change of source is communicated immediately and unequivocally to the stakeholders; the new one is clearly recognized by everyone thanks to public authentication by the former global source; and finally, the memory shared among them will allow those who remain—the new source as well as the collaborators—to publicly refer to it in the future, using their collective memory to go back to the well for some of that original source energy.

But it doesn't have to be a formal ritual—transmitting source works just as well when it's done informally. A face-to-face exchange at the office, for example, or in the car on the way home from an appointment. Once I even received a global source transmission (it was for a house) by telephone. The sole requirement for an effective informal transmission is that both donor and receiver agree, and express that to each other.

Everything I've said about how to transmit source applies to both horizontal and vertical transmission, albeit at different levels of intensity. Horizontally transmitting a part of the project field to a specific source is usually enacted informally, but there are times when a certain degree of formality could be preferable. In an engineering firm we work with, a team leader was struggling to inhabit her role. She realized that the firm's global source had never clearly notified her or her teammates that the specific source role for this team was being transmitted to her. When the unfortunate team leader finally spoke up, the global source was astonished: he'd been sure that the vague, casual allusion he thought he'd made had been enough to transmit source. ("When was that exactly?" asked the global source, who no longer even remembered it—a sure sign that the reality of the transfer was in doubt.) In that case, transmission failed to happen because the recipient didn't have the chance to agree to it. Logically enough, the confused team had trouble rallying round someone who was not the source. A little more formality would probably have helped all of them see their positions more clearly.

No matter the form, at the key moment the donor and the recipient of transmission find themselves together at a threshold, "a breach between time and space, between past and future, between inside and outside" (Sarthou-Lajus, 26). For this to happen, freedom must be present on both sides, and mutual trust. The risk is about to be taken, everyone is inwardly ready to abide by what will happen in the next moment—it's comparable to writing a blank cheque for whatever might happen in the future. On that threshold, with everything in place for the source to be passed, time seems to stand still until the moment the donor takes her last "next step". In that moment the receiver responds by taking his very first step in his new role: he accepts the source that is being passed to him.

A client told me about a great example of informal transfer—a transmission of global source he'd received some years earlier. On a Friday night, he was working late at the office after most of his co-workers had left for the weekend. Out of the blue, the company's global source, who was also its founder and general director (already past retirement age), appeared in his doorway—at the literal threshold! All he said was, "I think it's really time now for you to take over." And just like that, the source transmission was done.

But how to choose a successor? Many a source person is haunted by this—and with good reason. The question arises as soon as they realize that if they want their project, their movement, their business to survive after they're gone, they need to deal with their succession. Gotta find somebody. Whoever it is, what special qualities should they have? Many people automatically focus on the candidate's skill sets. Peter Koenig counters that *skills and competence are not determining factors* in the choice of a global source. Having some competence can undoubtedly be a plus, but it's far from essential—more like icing on the cake. Here again, the crucial thing is trust. As Sarthou-Lajus puts it so well, "the act of transmitting involves a relationship of trust that determines, regardless of our abilities or strengths, the meaning and value of what is transmitted. The quality of this relationship will make the transmission lively or moribund." (19). And where does this trust come from? From the current

global source's conviction that the future source will respect, care for and defend the project's core, its DNA: the project's vision, and its values. If the receiver doesn't actually share the vision and values that the donor conferred on the project (if she founded it), or recognizes in the project (if she's from a later source generation), he won't be able to become the global source—no matter how fantastic and perfectly aligned with the project his skill set might be.

On the other hand, no matter how few skills a future source might have in the project field, if he gets on board with the values and vision of the project because they correspond with his own, he can be an excellent global source. This happened to me when, even though I had no teaching degree, I opened a primary school and served as principal for almost a decade. If I'd been busy trying to get the right qualifications, I'd never have dared to do something like that. And don't forget: "We didn't know it was impossible—that's why we did it!" It goes without saying that skills are crucial to running a project, and this is exactly why the global source—who need not and cannot possess them all—invites specialists to join her project field and assume specific-source roles. But when you're researching a good candidate to transfer your global source to, the number one quality you're looking for is his ability to carry forward the values and drive the vision of the project against all odds.

And when you do transmit the global source, what is it that you're really transmitting? For one thing, as we saw in the preceding chapter, it's the *whole project* that's being passed to another person. Absolutely everything—the content of the project (its scope, achievements, resources, and its past and present), as well as its framework (its DNA, as expressed through values and vision). There is also transmission of a very subtle quality: knowing how to attract other people, a knack for spreading the global source's passion for her project.

This ineffable thing being transmitted does have some permanent aspects. Each new global source receives these unchanging features from her predecessor, and in time transmits them just as they are to her own successor—this is the source person's role as guardian, which she expresses through the conserving function of her authority (chapter 4). Other transmitted aspects can and should change along the way, in order to adjust the project to inevitable changes of context over time; here, the source person is exercising her role as guide, thanks to the differentiating function of her authority.

The essential and enduring element of what's transmitted is the *project field*. But far from being inert or fossilized, this permanence is in perpetual motion, constantly expanding and contracting, subject to the global source's widening or narrowing consciousness of what belongs to the project. And as long as there's a project, no matter how small, there's a project field. The sole unchanging element of the framework is its *values*, which the new source, fulfilling the role of guardian, is asked to retain just as he received them at the time of transmission. While his understanding of the project's values may evolve as he grasps their deeper meaning, the values themselves don't change over time.

But this is not so for the framework's other aspect, the *vision*—which is fundamentally dynamic. This means that the new global source has the power to adapt it to the various changes (whether these come from outside or inside) that will inevitably affect the project over time. In achieving the project's vision, the new source will above all exercise the roles of guide (defining the next steps) and entrepreneur (taking initiatives and risks).

The final thing being passed at transmission is *the ability to bring other people together* in the project. For every source person, past, present and future, this aptitude springs from her passion for her project. Every source person generates her own passion, a very personal reservoir of energy, and each one lives out that passion for the project in her own way, with varying degrees of intensity and fluency. The capacity to get people together, which the source-donor imperceptibly passes to the successor, is like a spark that fires up other people with the zeal and motivation of source. Any source person (global or specific) in good health—that is, not too afflicted with any of the source maladies—possesses an inner flame that generates the strength as source to pursue the project. And if this flame of passion should waver, her source channel is always there to revive the spark.

What happens if the succession fails? Let's pay careful attention to the words: it's true that a "failed" global- or specific-source succession—where the successor does not actually take on the responsibility of source—can and fairly often does happen. But the fact is that a source transmission, global or specific, can never "fail"—if it *seems* to have failed, then the gesture never happened and no transmission at all has occurred. This is the marvellous safety feature latent in the heart of every project: if a source person tries to transmit source to someone, and the candidate agrees verbally but doesn't really take it on (for whatever reason), the transmission did not happen and the project's source stays with the donor source person. This is why our projects, initiatives, businesses and relationships always have a "source person"—the old source just keeps functioning as such, with or without a title, until a new transmission enactment is organized and succeeds.

In a failed succession, the fault can lie with either side, or both. The receiver, for example, may have consented with his words, but not his heart, or have prematurely had to leave the project before he could truly inhabit his source role. As for the donor, she could have imagined (consciously or not) that transmission took place, even though in reality she hadn't managed to separate herself from the project's source and stayed too attached to "her" project. I used to know the elderly founder of a charity, a man who for many years had given everything to a life's work. His multiple attempts to transmit source had all been aborted, with considerable suffering by the replacement candidates who ultimately were all rejected. Eventually he found himself faced with the very suitable choice of a tall, strapping fellow who gained his trust and put himself forward at the right moment to accurately negotiate the conditions of transfer. I was present at their enactment of source transmission during a general assembly, and was happy that the founder had finally found the strength to let go. A few years later I heard from the new source that in the period following this transmittal, the founder had tried to rescind some elements of the transfer, but his attempt failed: once source is handed over, it's been transmitted, and the former source can't take it back unless his successor decides, freely, to give back the *whole* project.

Up to this point, we've been looking at source transmissions where the source person is directly responsible for choosing a successor. But as in many public and private collectives today, what happens when the global source's participation is excluded by the executive board's appointment process? Sometimes it seems that these organizations make it a point of honour to prevent the source person from choosing a successor with the excuse that this will help instigate "change". When it's a case of replacing a specific source, there's no problem—that task falls naturally to the global source of the project field, so the specific source has no need to participate (although it would be possible, as we have seen, with the consent of the global source). But a genuine global source cannot be replaced during his or her lifetime without at least being able to consent to the choice of a successor. And don't forget: "global source" can't be hijacked, it can only be given.

In fact, this problem of exclusion arises from the board's significant misunderstanding of the difference between, on the one hand, the outgoing person's role of source, and on the other, her job as manager-in-charge. Usually the outgoing global source is excluded from the nomination process not so much because of her role as source (the ultimate responsible person), but rather because of her role as manager-in-charge (who must be replaced and therefore doesn't need to be included in the nomination process). Generally, the "deciders" (members of the executive board, for example, or board of trustees) completely ignore the distinction between *managerial functions* (which they do have the power to appoint) and *source role* (which only the current global source can transmit). So they may in good faith try to replace the executive director without understanding that she is also the global source. The organization then finds itself in a difficult situation where the new executive director has taken over his predecessor's duties, but without having received the global source. This situation has nothing to recommend it, neither for the executive director who has been awarded a "mission impossible", nor for the organization—which, since it no longer benefits from the global source's intuition and insights regarding next steps, will find itself deprived of its future and in the long run will cease to exist.

As a matter of fact, there is a solution to this difficulty, but it depends entirely on how well the global source can harness the conditions of source transmission (free choice, trust, and willingness to take risks) even while she's left out of the appointment process. I accompanied a boss who was close to retirement, whose fairly large business was part of an even bigger entity. Although his business was more or less independent of the larger company, he'd been excluded (as was the rule) from choosing his own successor—with the board of directors disregarding the idea of source. After he and I reflected together on the situation, we understood that, even if they excluded him from choosing his successor, he could still transmit the project's global source to another person providing he *trusted* her. As trust can only be born and nurtured when people know each other, it was imperative that he be able to work with his successor (an external candidate). So he made a proposal to the board (here's the risk-taking): to hire the successor three months prior to his own actual departure, so the two of them could work together to transfer the files. At the end of the quarter, the global source, now reassured, decided (and here's the freedom to choose) to transmit the source to his successor. The board didn't know anything about his tactics to get the source properly transferred… I imagine if and when the new global source reads this, she will be grateful to the outgoing source for cleverly circumventing the obstacle to the succession, for the greater good of the company and the incoming global source's success in her new job.

Before reading further, try this: question your own organization's rules for appointing senior positions. Do they take the role of source person into account?

What would have happened to the global source in the previous example, if he *hadn't* trusted his replacement and had freely chosen not to transmit the source? In that case, the former manager would have still been the global source, but after his departure he would no longer have been part of the business. This would have greatly complicated his responsibilities as source, but in a situation like this, how could he manage, from outside, to access sufficient confidential-yet-essential information on the company's operations to recognize its current challenges? And if he did have enough knowledge to advance his source reflection on what the next step should be, how could he communicate this clarity to his collaborators? How could he ensure that the project framework (vision and values) would be respected by all, and drive everyone's attitudes and choices? How to take care of the project field, and at the same time fulfil his responsibilities as global source within every section he'd entrusted to specific sources?

When the global source is physically located outside the project, whether she likes it or not, she remains intimately bound, as source person, to the core of the project—and continues to carry full responsibility for it. This opens up the real risk that she will develop the "slacker" pathology, neglecting the source work that needs to be done (chapter 3). Or she might succumb to a malady that's not so much "source denier" as "source denied", in that the project participants no longer recognize her as the source. An organization that doesn't know who its global source is, even though there definitely is one, will never know where to go next or how to get there. Without an active global source, it will inevitably go into decline and, ultimately, disappear.

Clearly, it's far from ideal to be a global source located outside your project. In the end, it can only work if the global source can count on a base, or staging post, at the project's core. Peter Koenig calls this link the "source representative", who functions as a bridge between the global source and her project. This usually arises spontaneously, without the conscious intention of either the source or the representative: they simply pursue the good collegial and friendly relations they had before, because they instinctively feel the project's ongoing need for them to be connected with each other. Of course, the representative's task is far from easy, and sourcing a project through an intermediary is also not ideal. But under the circumstances it allows the project to at least survive, to continue despite the source's absence.

In the rare instance where the global source is aware of the problem right from the start (this is a lot easier if she's familiar with source principles) she can seek out a good representative on her own. This stand-in must not only hold enough of a key position to have access to information, he must also be able to exert sufficient influence on the project's movement, keep the global source informed about what's happening, and above all be able to communicate the clarifications he's received from her about the next steps. In other words, in his capacity as her spokesperson, the representative helps the global source keep the project alive. But Peter Koenig reports that it's unfortunately much more frequent for a global source who's left her project's official organization (especially if she's been ejected) to sincerely believe she's no longer in the loop and so doesn't consider enlisting someone from her inner circle to be her source representative. In that case, however, a person within the project who sees signs that the initiative is drifting into troubled waters can step up and volunteer to be the source's representative. That person can take the initiative to contact the global source and ask her about the project's next steps. This would supply him with missing vital information to be passed on to the project's actors, enabling them to get the project back on course.

One last word on transmitting source within a couple. In chapter 5 we looked at how various source relationships—sometimes global, sometimes specific—develop within their reciprocal give and take. As we saw, one of them, by taking the initiative and the first risk, has become the *global source* of their relationship, whereas the other, in accepting the invitation, has made them a couple—and is in fact the *specific source* of the relationship. But it sometimes happens that the responsibility for developing the relationship becomes too burdensome for the global source. One of the participants in a training course on source principles had had a serious illness that obliged him to mobilize all his energy to heal. Though unacquainted with source vocabulary, this global source of their relationship initiated a profound dialogue about their situation. Together, they decided that she, not he, would now be responsible for the evolution of their relationship. So they transferred global source—in other words they switched the roles of global and specific source, making the unwell spouse the specific source of their relationship. After he recovered, they left things as they were: the transfer had worked out very well for both of them.

Of course, transmitting source isn't limited to exchanging the global source of the relationship (along with its source responsibilities); you can also switch around whatever other source roles you've developed over time. As we understand more about how source responsibilities get transferred and how to give and take source roles in couples, maybe there will be fewer divorces?

# Chapter 9

## *Cast your bread upon the waters*

---

FINALLY, let's move on to another form of transmission—not of source itself, but of the principles that govern it. Perhaps reading this book has given you a glimpse of the abundant riches within the idea of source, and you might have sensed that for understanding your own responsibilities—in your tasks, your projects and your life—source principles can be highly relevant. Now you may feel more connected to your own source, and it has taken on significance in your eyes—if so, then a great way of acknowledging that would be to share the experience with people you live and work with. "*Bonum diffusivum sui*", or "Good stuff spreads by itself"*, as the saying inspired by Plato goes (*Timaeus*, 29d-30a). If you've read this far, you'll probably agree that being aware of source principles, and trying to use them, is really something good, so you'll naturally want to pass them on—it's why I wrote the book in the first place! When it comes to source principles, when we are filled, we well up, we overflow.

So why not take a chance and pass along the source principles in situations where they might help move things forward? In our businesses, organizations, projects and relationships the source principles can help clarify who's responsible for what, so each person has a place that fits. These principles can help us see how our pathologies handicap us, and support us in overcoming them. They prompt us to put more creativity and dedication into setting the course for our project's future. In the collective, they allow us to better understand the role of the individual— and to take that understanding into account as we work together. And for future source persons, the source principles will boost their courage, empowering them to take the necessary initiatives and risks to turn their intuitions into reality.

Maybe you've met people who seem to emanate goodwill—it just seems to flow out of them. Transmitting source principles works like that, and its intent is the opposite of indoctrination. As Nathalie Sarthou-Lajus explains it, indoctrination is meant to "make another identical to oneself through coercion", whereas successful transmission always presupposes freedom of choice: it's "all about acquiring the ability to choose and individual freedom" (*Le geste de transmettre,* 99). Source principles themselves are based on this fundamental freedom, which is expressed in each of our initiatives and risks, in each step forward, and in each successful transmission of source. If source principles are easy to pass along, it's because

they deeply resonate with our life experiences. They give us a common vocabulary for discussion, helping to ease the conversation back and forth between theory and practice, between conceptual frameworks and concrete experience. Talking about source principles to yourself and to other people whenever you think it could shed light on what's happening—isn't that the best way to spread the good stuff around? So I think we can all be grateful to Peter Koenig for creating this source language and letting us know about it.

Disseminating source principles is an individual responsibility, but it also has a collective dimension. Let's make sure our management role models are "source-compatible".

Several new participatory management and governance models have recently been applied in our companies and institutions, notably Freedom, Inc., Evolutionary-Teal Organizations, Sociocracy, Holacracy®, participatory dynamics, and so on. I'm convinced that they will flourish only if they incorporate source principles in order to balance the dual aims of legitimately reducing the weight of the hierarchy with the necessity of respecting source persons' responsibilities. In the participatory dynamics we transmit at Ordinata we emphasize this balance, and the method has inevitably gained greater depth, coherence and influence from the moment we first integrated the source principles. In the coming decade, other methodologies will surely follow, encouraged by the example of Frédéric Laloux\* who, in the video follow-up to his book, *Reinventing Organizations*, progressively introduces the notion of source. Since a language now exists to express and share source principles, it will be difficult for any serious collaborative method to ignore them for long. This is one more reason to disseminate them widely.

In the early years of this century Peter Koenig started transmitting the rudiments of this source language. Thanks to input from the many people who value it, the source principles vocabulary and grammar have been greatly enriched. The language development process is still going on, and each one of us is invited to participate in its evolution. The more we expand our understanding of source principles and experience how they work, the better we'll be able to communicate them. Remember—the best way to broadcast something is to live it! So let's support each other to be wholly source in our initiatives, activities, and relationships.

# Epilogue

## *Principles of love*

---

BEFORE we complete the voyage that this little red book has taken us on, let's move out into the open sea. So far, we've been carried through different currents: welcoming source, sharing it with others and passing it on. This source itinerary represents the comings and goings of our own lives: welcoming, sharing, transmitting.

To live your source is an exhilarating experience whose main dimensions are personal accomplishment and giving. Or could we go so far as to say personal fulfilment *through* giving? By listening to his or her intuitions, taking initiatives and risks, creating a collective around an idea, and continually clarifying next steps, the source person is in fact responding to a profound motivation, a call from inside—the call of source. This is what gives meaning to our actions and our very existence: being source is a genuine way to take care of ourselves, to find joy and have a rich, full life. At the same time, the source person only achieves this personal fulfilment by sparing no effort to realize his or her initiative, taking care not only of the project but also of the individuals and the collective helping to accomplish it. "Giving" is not just an empty word: it means responding concretely to that inner call, aligning your actions with it, actualizing yourself by sharing what you're filled with—like an abundantly overflowing spring. In the end, a source person can only be completely *source* by giving.

To give is to love! In becoming fully source—whether of a humble idea or a grand project—I enter into the dynamics of achieving and giving, of abundance and abandonment: a powerful way of loving. That's why as a source person I love my project, I love the people in it and, revelling in the sense of meaning and accomplishment that comes from exercising my role as source, I love myself. In the end, we can feel assured that the source principles are *principles of love*.

As philosophers say, "Love goes after what it thinks is good".* In other words, when I love something or someone, I always think it's good for me. What's good for a source person? Seeing your initiative develop, your project succeed, your company prosper, your relationship flourish—all this completes you. Your "good" is this: your vision is realized and your actions reflect your values. Through this gift of love, the source person makes it all happen—it's a wonderful expression of passion for your project.

But love can be hard. A source person can easily be tempted to follow the mighty ego and become a counterfeit source, a tyrant, or to slip recklessly downhill toward those careless figures we called source denier and slacker. These maladies generate a domination-submission relationship—not just between the source person and the project, but also between the source and the individuals in the collective. When the collective is a couple, this can be painfully obvious… These pathologies inevitably lead the source person to use others as the means to an end, something *taken* but not welcomed—and this is emphatically not love's logic. Sure, it's great to be of use to others, and to consider others as being useful—but only as long as we remember that the other is a person, an end in herself, who we can't really love if we've instrumentalized her as the means to an end. This what the ethicist Karol Wojtyla\* is saying when he claims that "love is the opposite of using". Here we are touching on a fundamental condition of the source person's role: to work unremittingly to detect and mitigate his own "fake source" attitudes, especially his failure to give—so that day by day he moves ever closer to the side of love.

Recognizing the source principles, and living them, can take us to all kinds of places. Though no one is obliged to follow them, the conscious exercise of source principles just might lead us—as we've already seen—to reflect upon and experience things that touch on the realm of spirituality. Every source person will eventually ask questions like: *Where do all these intuitions, inspirations and ideas that generate my role as source come from? This energy to make my initiatives happen, where does it come from? What's at the other end of my 'source channel'?* Indeed, intuiting that my source itself has a Source, as Lytta Basset would put it\*, could be the starting point of a "quest for the Source" (with a capital "S"), discovering unexpected horizons. It's a spiritual journey where everyone is invited. Depending on your motivation and means, come along at your own speed.

Before I give the word over to Peter Koenig, you deserve an answer to the question of colour: why is this little book red? Maybe the title reminds you of Chairman Mao's *Little Red Book*\*, or even of C.G. Jung's *Red Book*. While *A little red book about source* is obviously neither a political manifesto nor a psychological disquisition, you may have sensed there is indeed something revolutionary embedded here: if everybody started to consciously live out these source principles, the face of the world would never be the same again.

Perhaps blue—the colour of water—might have been better for a book about source? But isn't red the colour of desire, of energy, of giving, of love? Red's deep associations with source don't end there: red commands us to act and also to stop, it stands for blood and for the sacred, for passion and for life. It's the colour of the heart. Is there a more sublime way to signify that source principles are principles of love? Anything is possible as long as there are courageous source persons to stand up and take new initiatives—and to love!

May the source-current flow freely through every one of your projects, properties, relationships and dreams—making them glow, flare up and thrive.

And now, let's get busy with our sources…

# Afterword by Peter John Koenig

## *Changing times*

IT'S not just a cliché but has become clear that we're living in a time of great changes. As a 71-year-old who has been consciously following these developments for more than half a lifetime, it seems to me that the changes have only just begun.

Looking at the world today, I admit it would be easy to become a pessimist. But having had the great gift and privilege to get in touch with why I was born, my deep belief is that whoever gets to this point, lives content with (or despite) their circumstances, then dies, and if there's an afterlife, lives happily ever after.

My faith in this comes from deep within. But as our consciousness evolves, the circumstances and problems that confront us may not just shrink as we hope, but actually become larger… because our capacity to deal with them also grows apace! Looking ahead now at future prospects this outcome seems very probable. So while I find no grounds for unrealistic optimism based on what's happening presently, I also find none for unrealistic pessimism.

From this perspective my own calling pulled me as a young man to research and develop from scratch what I call "moneywork", originally a system designed to understand and align one's relation to money, but which has since become a way of accelerating personal growth in general. Much later and almost by surprise I fell upon a sideline that has since become equally important to me—the "sourcework" you've just been reading about. Equally important because if moneywork enables an increasingly frequent and strong connection to one's inner source, the sourcework will, I hope, provide an equivalent acceleration in the realization of good projects and initiatives in the world outside, with an exponentially growing number of increasingly enlightened sources.

It's in this context that I'm deeply grateful to Stefan Merckelbach for his contribution in authoring and bringing out this first major written work on source. Not only does it contain an accurate description of what I've been working on these last years, with a beautiful overlay and elaboration of his own expression, but *A little red book about source* is itself an embodiment of the source principles described within it. Over the years, as thousands of people have confirmed and reconfirmed these source principles in their own lives, I'm occasionally accused of having become too dogmatic about them. I find the gentle, sensitive and step-by-step approach that Stefan has used to introduce and explain them, exemplary. I could not wish for better or more.

In deepest appreciation then, wishing you the reader, no matter what your age, profession, politics or other persuasion, much love and success in the realization of all your deepest wishes. May you also live happily ever after!

Peter John Koenig
*December 2018*

# Vincent Delfosse

## *Images and words of source*

FROM the mountain pass, the source I chose is a gleam before it's even a murmur. Reflecting the autumn sun, it drizzles the mountainside with bright veins of light. I follow it down, as eager to meet it as to unload my rucksack.

There where it's silent (is it the mountain or the water that picks the spot?) it offers itself to the sky above with a slow shiver from beneath the shade of a rock wall. If not for the way it eddies down the first slope, I could almost doubt this skimpy stream, this promise of a torrent. I fill my water bottle, drink, then follow its moves: at the smallest stone, at every startled babble, there it is, talking with the mountain. Gurgling, onomatopoeia and serenades intermingled. I let myself be guided by the sound of its voice. Listening to the source-stream, I step over it a hundred times. In some places it even disappears under a carpet of stones—beclouding its path and stirring up mystery. Further on it's joined by the water of tributaries, then picks out detours edged with bulrushes. To me it's beautiful.

Of course, as it becomes more conspicuous the river gets a name on the map, conferred by men lacking landmarks or intimacy with it. But we're not quite there yet. First I want to hear its given name, the one for this encounter where my attention veers between keeping my ears open, framing a picture, and listening to what this canvas awakens in me: an ancient peace, a freedom rooted in the mountain, a visceral, wild enchantment. Yes, its eloquence is made of water, minerals and life. Just like me. In a way, my pictures are in pursuit of this echo. Now the alpenglow (a photographer's dream) is slip-sliding into night. I unroll my sleeping bag. From here at ground level the river's song is undetectable. The mist joins me in this moonlight-whitened silence.

Awakened by the cold, I play at believing the river has disappeared. I rise in the night and take a few steps to find its voice again. Under the stars its sounds are mutating into other words. It's watching. I fall back to sleep as far as my fatigue and the cold will let me.

The new day (or why not "this unique day") arrives with the sun as a natural extension of the night. I walk the shore of a small alpine lake where the river widens. Lapping waves, some tiny frogs, there are still some polliwogs. Then the lake becomes waterfall, thudding crash, force of gravity.

Hours of walking downstream, and abruptly there's a ground catchment. Concrete, its destiny utilitarian, a dotted line on the map. Further down, the water flows wordlessly into the ancestral watercourse, restored for tourism with great fanfare, plastic tarps and metal sheets. The river, tamed by mechanized locks, almost forgets its name and is lost in silence. I think of digitized voices, the ones everywhere that announce public transport stops, erasing accents and shredding place names. Man sighs, source sighs. The peak and yesterday's first gleam of light seem very far away, and my walker's legs agree.

I leave with pictures bearing witness to the sound of its voice, and when I look them over on the return train, I anticipate showing them to Stefan, overjoyed to contribute to this little book (it's far from finished, one knows only that it will be red), because these principles so often enlighten me and thrust me along in my own projects.

In my water bottle—in my veins—there's still a little river water. In my words, a bit of that voice. I'll go back to recharge, to re-source up there, time and again to overhear its call, rain or shine: dare to create, free and alive!

Vincent Delfosse, www.verschez.com

*Col de la Tsevalire, unnamed spring 2658 m.*
*Lac du Louché, along the river La Rèche*
*Canton of Valais, October 2018*

# Acknowledgements

## *Another source adventure*

*A little red book about source* was first published in French in 2019, and then in German in Spring 2020. When the time came to offer it in Peter John Koenig's mother tongue, it was he, the "father" of the source principles, who suggested Karen Smith, an old friend of his who's also based in Zurich, to do the English translation.

Our first meeting took place on October 24, 2019, at the Limattquai in Zurich, in the Café *Franzos*. I had deliberately chosen the place for its name: it seemed the right starting point for a translation project of a book written in «Franzos» (meaning *French* in the Zurich dialect). Karen Smith had often spoken with Peter Koenig about the source principles, so she was already well aware of their importance, and after our first meeting she agreed to translate a chapter and give it a try. I soon discovered

Karen Smith's profoundly intelligent and strong personality, constantly trying to find the most appropriate and powerful way to express the source principles in English, with the greatest possible economy of words and fidelity to the French original.

We quickly decided on our working method, which combined videoconferencing for our text revisions with online files, allowing both of us simultaneous access to the translations. We hadn't set ourselves a binding agenda, but thought we had departed on a long journey when the imposition of Covid-19 confinement "trapped" her in Southern France. At the same time, it obliged my company in Switzerland, Ordinata, to suspend all its workshops and group trainings for several months. From one day to the next, the situation gave both of us that commodity which has become so rare in our normally overbooked lives: time! Our Zoom meetings proliferated and before we knew it, we'd gone through all the chapters. Then we did everything over again and again, to sharpen the text and enable a more fluent read. During the more than 30 virtual encounters we had together, I can't count the times we burst out laughing when Karen's sense of humour detected something funny, the moments of semi-despair when our search for the right word seemed to come up against insurmountable incompatibility between the language of Molière and that of Shakespeare, the sighs of relief and joy when our perseverance gave birth to a good solution.

Little by little, Karen Smith really tuned in to the voice and the message of the book, becoming in her turn a source by enriching it with new images, sounds and colours that would make the source principles even more accessible to an English-speaking audience. This is how the Beatles, or even Ikea furniture discreetly entered into the text. Karen has also improved many passages with her edits, constantly questioning me about their meaning and helping me rewrite them. In short, she has greatly improved this book with her many initiatives... and risks, in the face of my too-well-known lack of flexibility! I can't tell her—and you—enough how grateful I am to her for having put so much passion, energy and skill into the adventure, and I consider myself very lucky to have gained a dear friend in the process.

In the final phase before publication, four more people have been of great support in proofreading and correcting this translation and giving feedback on their experience as first readers: Tash Stallard for a start, from Unassuming Radicals in the U.K. (www.unassumingradicals.com), a friend of mine among the Peter Koenig master class alumni, who applies the source principles in her professional activity and knows a lot about it. Then came Jane Reed and Andrew Barrs, colleagues of Karen Smith, who brought their unbiased, critical minds to their reading. Their "test-driving" has helped to improve the readers' experience of this book. And Peter Koenig himself has done a final reading of *A little red book about source* in English, to ensure that the translation you are holding in your hands is consistent with its original. Many thanks to all these people for their invaluable help!

Just before completing these pages, Peter Koenig has written to me that my acknowledgements would be incomplete if they failed to include one more person. This is Robert Hargrove of the Relationships Organization and Hargrove Associates, author of the book *Masterful Coaching*. It was from Robert Hargrove that Peter first heard the word "source" applied to the founder of an organization. And it was through Robert Hargrove's Relationships Workshop with Gervaise Boucher in May 1981 that Peter met Karen Smith, and then brought Andrew Barrs into their team. Their friendship and collaboration have been very much in line with the practicality and natural beauty of these source principles. Without Robert Hargrove's originating place in the source lineage of this book, and Peter Koenig's nearly four decades of thorough reflection and unflagging research on source, I would not have written these lines and you would not be reading them.

As soon as Karen Smith is back in Zurich and this book begins to reach its English-speaking readers, where will we go to celebrate the completion of our project? After the *Franzos* where our adventure began, wouldn't it be more appropriate to opt this time for an Anglophile establishment? Will it be the *James Joyce Pub*, or rather *The Brisket Southern BBQ*? Or simply *Just Soup*? Source doubts, there we go again!

Stefan Merckelbach
*August 2020*

# *Resources*

## Source principles—first sightings in print

The very first article on source principles is by **Nadjeschda Taranczewski** in January 2014: "The Role of Source in Organizations": *The Mobius Strip Magazine* (Winter 2014): 55-57. In October 2015 she published an updated version, "Who's Idea Was it Anyway? The Role of Source in Organizations": medium.com/@AhoiNadjeschda/who-s-idea-was-it-any-way-the-role-of-source-in-organizations-843b407e2879.

The first published book chapter on the source person is in French, by the inspiring Canadian retirement consultant **Martine Deschamps**: *Planifier sa retraite ou sa relève… ça ne fait pas mourir!* (Plan your retirement or succession—it won't kill you!), (Un monde différent 2017), 95-110.

**Graham Duncan** gives interesting testimony about source in Timothy Ferriss's book, *Tribe of Mentors: Short life advice from the best in the* *world* (Houghton Mifflin Harcourt, 2017), 58-59.

**Frédéric Laloux**, in his summarized version of *Reinventing Organizations: An illustrated invitation to join the conversation on next-stage organizations* (illustrated by Étienne Appert: Nelson Parker 2016), discusses Peter Koenig's source principles (note 20, 164-165). In his video sequel to *Reinventing Organizations*, he fleshes out his initial remarks, convincingly introducing the role of the source person (see video 1.10 "Your roles in this new world" of the series "Insights for the Journey", https://thejourney.reinventingorganizations.com/110.html).

**Tom Nixon** has recently published *Work with Source*: *A handbook for movement leaders and purpose-driven entrepreneurs* (Summer 2020), a great contribution, based on Peter Koenig's research, to help source persons realize big ideas, organize for participation, work artfully with money, and let it go when they're done. This inspirational and very practical book is divided in four parts: Creative Fields, Creative Flow, Creative Organising, Creative Money. To be ordered at www.workwithsource.com.

# Reading notes

**On the threshold** (11-13) — **workwithsource.com** is a platform promoting the source principles used by the consultancy and research community around Peter John Koenig. The driving forces behind the website are Charlie Davies (charlesdavies.com) and, more recently, Tom Nixon (tomnixon.co.uk; see his book *Work with Source* on the previous page).

For **Peter Koenig**'s "moneywork" see his blog, peterkoenig.typepad.com.

**Chapter 2** (25-39) — **"intuition"** and **"source channel"**: Having received *A little red book about source* in its original French edition, out of the blue my niece Carla Houben (mintmediations.nl) sent me a copy of Joseph Jaworski's book with the very evocative title *Source: The Inner Path of Knowledge Creation* (Berrett-Koehler Publishers 2012). I was thrilled to discover many striking thoughts parallel to those of Peter Koenig, about intuition, source channels and much more, which had all emerged during Jaworski's research with Otto Scharmer and other MIT colleagues on the theory of learning and management called "Theory U". In this inspiring theory, the notion of "Source" is linked to the "bottom of the U", that specific place where, through a process of letting go of everything inessential, a subtle connection is established to a deeper source of knowing. Throughout his book *Source*, Joseph Jaworski seeks to answer these two fundamental questions: "What is the *source* [his italics] of our capacity to access the knowledge for action we need in the moment? How can we learn to enable that capacity, individually and collectively?" (2).

**Chapter 3** (41-54) — "**external objective or internal intention?**" In my 2017 book on Ordinata (in French and in German) I called for management by intention instead of (the still too popular) management by objectives. Intention, like source, springs from within the person and is much more motivating and efficient than an objective, which is always situated outside the person (imposed by her or someone else). See *Le dit d'Ordinata: réflexions sur l'exercice d'un métier insolite*, 2nd edition (Aquilae Editions 2017), 29-33.

**Chapter 4** (59-72) — The "**reciprocal causality of total causes**" is masterfully described by André de Muralt, a Swiss philosopher who was my professor in Mediaeval Philosophy at Geneva University, in *L'Enjeu de la Philosophie Médiévale* (E. J. Brill 1991).

The three-dimensional notion of "**authority**" is detailed by Ariane Bilheran in *L'Autorité. Psychologie et psychopathologie* (Armand Colin 2016). She borrows it from Myriam Revault d'Allonnes' very interesting book, *Le Pouvoir des commencements. Essais sur l'autorité* (Seuil 2006), which presents in particular the way power and space correlate with authority and time. Revault d'Allones explains that authority is not the same as power, but is defined in relation to it. It is deployed in time and duration, while power comes into play with the sharing of space. Authority is a fundamental dimension of the social bond because it ensures transmission, filial relationship and the continuity of generations, while staying vigilant towards the crises that threaten to tear at its web. Both authors draw heavily on Hannah Arendt's work on authority and power.

**Chapter 5** (73-84) — It's interesting to see how **Frédéric Laloux**'s thinking has evolved. In his *Reinventing Organizations: A guide to creating organizations inspired by the next stage of human consciousness* (Nelson Parker 2014) he's still ignoring source principles, even though the founders and executive directors he interviews for his study on "Evolutionary-Teal Organizations" are each, in fact, the global source of their respective organizations. Then, having taken part in a source principles seminar, he becomes aware of them, integrating them little by little into his own vision of a new management paradigm (see above under "Source principles—first sightings in print").

**Chapter 7** (99-110) — **Nathalie Sarthou-Lajus**'s inspiring book about enacting transmission, *Le geste de transmettre* (Bayard 2017), wonderfully describes the phenomenology of transmission. She is cited throughout this book (including in chapters 8 & 9).

In **Martine Deschamps**' *Planifier sa retraite ou sa relève…ça ne fait pas* *mourir!* (Un monde différent 2017), there's an entire chapter on the question of identifying the source of a company (95-110). It presents several concrete cases of source transmission and underlines the importance of preparing well for the transfer of source. The author nicely describes specific sources as "resources".

**Chapter 9** (129-133) — "**Bonum diffusivum sui**" or "**Good stuff spreads by itself**": This principle turns up repeatedly across the history of Western philosophy, from Plato (5$^{th}$ century BC) to Thomas Aquinas (13$^{th}$ century AD). We could also translate it as "Good communicates itself". This force of diffusion of good has always fascinated me; the more we give, the more there is! Isn't this just like source, which gushes out without stopping?

**Frédéric Laloux**, see above note under chapter 5.

**Epilogue** (135-139) — "**Love goes after what it thinks is good**" stems from the venerable philosophical maxim "the good is the proper cause of love": This formulation comes from Thomas Aquinas's 13$^{th}$-century *Summa Theologica* I-II, 27 art. 1, response (see https://www.newadvent.org/summa/2027.htm), but the same idea can be found in Aristotle and St. Augustine.

In 1960, **Karol Wojtyla** (the future Pope John Paul II) developed, in his book *Love and Responsibility* (New English Translation, Pauline Books

& Media 2013), his "personalist norm" which he says is the basis of the statement "love is the opposite of using". According to him, the person is a "good" towards which the only appropriate and valid attitude is love. Therefore, it would be unjust to use a person as a means. Moreover, the theme of "giving oneself" is of great importance in his work; he derived it from this Vatican II statement: "Man [...] cannot fully find himself except through a sincere gift of himself." (*Gaudium et Spes* 24:3).

**Lytta Basset** develops the "intuition of a Source" and the "quest for the Source" in *La Source que je cherche* (Albin Michel 2017, 24 and 10).

In western languages, Mao's **Little Red Book** is a commonly used way of referring to Quotations from Chairman Mao Tse-Tung. It originally came out in Chinese in 1964. C. J. Jung's *Red Book* was written and illustrated by the famous Swiss psychoanalyst between 1913 and 1930, but remained unpublished until 2009.

## Trainings and consulting on source principles

Several English-speaking trainers and coaches briefly introduce themselves on the site **workwithsource.com/people**, under the heading "People". You can contact them from there.

Ordinata, the company of which Stefan Merckelbach is the global source, offers several ways of integrating the source principles. Working in French, German, English and Italian, Stefan and his team present trainings, professionnal Co-development groups, source workshops and individual source support (both online and in person) in Givisiez, Switzerland, and elsewhere on request: **www.alittleredbookaboutsource.com/sourcework**.

*A little red book about source*:
**Order more copies at www.alittleredbookaboutsource.com**, on the main Internet platforms, or from your bookseller. Offering the book to your colleagues, friends and family is a great way to spread the word.

Share your personal experience of the source principles with other readers at **www.alittleredbookaboutsource.com/sourcestories**.

# Index

## A

ability to bring other people together in the project 119
added value as a source person 51
Arendt, Hannah 157
Aristotle 53, 66, 158
art of "we" 76, 82
Augustine, St. 158
authority 47, 68-71, 80, 88, 90, 100, 118, 156, 157
- conserving function of 70, 118
- differentiating function of 70, 118
- generating function of 70

## B

Barrs, Andrew 151, 152
Basset, Lytta 138, 159
Beatles, the 51, 151
Bilheran, Ariane 70, 156
Boucher, Gervaise 152

## C

cascade of sources 29, 62, 64-66
cash 28
channel, source channel 20, 32, 34, 119, 138, 155
children (source of their arrival) 17, 83
clarity about the next step 31-34, 62, 81-82, 93, 112, 124
Co-development 160
*Col de la Tsevalire* 147
collective 38, 59, 72, 73-84, 85, 90, 93-94, 102, 109, 112, 113, 130, 132, 135, 136, 137
collective intelligence 33, 76, 79, 93, 94
communicate clarity 26, 29, 33-34, 44, 52, 81, 124, 125, 133
competence 41, 76, 84, 115-117
couple 82-84, 102, 126-127, 137

Covid-19  150
creativity  20, 21, 130
cultural change  109
culture  37, 64, 75

## D

Davies, Charles  155
decision by consent  79-81
Delfosse, Vincent  145-147
Deschamps, Martine  107, 153, 157
dialogue  31, 32-33, 34, 35, 36, 37, 44, 51, 79, 93, 112, 126
dictator (source person as)  46
DNA of the project  37, 39, 107, 117, 118
domination-submission relationship  137
doubt  31, 44, 114, 145
Duncan, Graham  153
dynamiqueparticipative.be  76

## E

ego  46-49, 53, 69, 71, 137
energy  11, 20, 27, 34, 42, 50-51, 53-54, 60-61, 69, 71, 75, 86-87, 91, 93, 94, 104, 107, 109, 113, 119, 126, 137, 138, 151
entrepreneur (source role as)  26, 27-34, 43, 60, 61, 64, 66, 68, 70, 71, 82, 101, 102, 119
equivalency, principle of  80-82
*ergon*  25, 26, 41, 52
Evolutionary-Teal Organizations  132, 157

## F

Ferriss, Timothy  153
field of awareness  69
field (source field, project field)  49, 60-71, 73, 74, 79, 83, 88, 90, 91, 93, 94, 100, 104-108, 113, 117, 118, 121, 124
first step  25, 28, 31, 114

fragility of source  26
Freedom, Inc.  132
freedom, liberty  20, 21, 101, 104, 105, 110, 114, 123, 130, 146
friendship  17, 92, 152
future source  117, 130

## G

giving, gift of self  29, 31, 69, 101, 102, 135-139, 151, 159
global source  20, 60-72, 73, 74, 75, 77, 80, 81, 82, 83, 85, 88, 90, 91, 92, 99-110, 111-127, 157, 160
good  129, 158
guardian (source role as)  26, 35-39, 43, 60, 61, 64, 66, 68, 70, 71, 82, 92, 101, 118
guide (source role as)  26, 28-34, 35, 39, 43, 60, 61, 64, 66, 68, 70, 71, 82, 101, 118, 119, 157

## H

Hargrove, Robert 68, 151, 152
Hemmer, Pierre 62
hierarchy 65, 66, 77, 79, 81, 132
Holacracy® 132
Houben, Carla 155
house (source of a) 61, 71, 75, 113
humility 18, 112

## I

idea 17-20, 21, 25, 27, 31, 32, 33, 35, 36, 37, 39, 41, 43, 52, 59, 60, 62, 68, 73, 74, 86, 88, 90, 92, 110, 112, 122, 123, 129, 135, 136, 153, 155, 158, 159
ideas are gifts 18
Ikea 25, 151
initiative 17-18, 20, 21, 22, 25, 26, 27, 28, 29, 35, 36, 37, 39, 42, 43, 44, 46, 48, 50, 51, 52, 53, 54, 59, 60, 61, 69, 70, 74, 77, 82, 83, 86, 88, 90, 91, 92, 100, 101, 105, 106, 109, 126, 136
investment 28

## J

Jobs, Steve 49
joy of source 52, 54, 112, 136
Jung, Carl Gustav 138, 159

## K

Koenig, Peter John 11, 12, 13, 20, 21, 22, 27, 34, 38, 42, 46, 60, 65, 66, 68, 69, 82, 86, 87, 90, 91, 94, 108, 115, 125, 132, 133, 138, 143, 149, 151, 152, 154, 155

## L

*Lac du Louché* 147
Laloux, Frédéric 77, 132, 154, 157, 158
*La Rèche* 147
*Le dit d'Ordinat*a 156
*little red book about source, A* 12, 135, 138, 142, 149, 151, 155, 160
*Little Red Book* (Mao) 138, 159
love 46, 135-138, 143, 158, 159
- love as the opposite of using 137, 159
- principles of love 135, 136, 138

## M

management 75, 77, 79, 80, 132, 155, 156, 157
- management by objectives or intention 156
managerial function 122
Mao Tse-Tung 138, 159
Maptio, maptio.com 65
Marenne, Martine 13, 76, 93, 99
master class (of Peter Koenig) 11, 13, 151

moneywork  142, 155
motivation  21, 34, 50, 87, 95, 109, 119, 135, 138
Muralt, André de  156

## N

Neri, Philip  48
nested circles  65
next step  28-34, 41, 43, 44, 52, 65, 67, 79, 81, 93, 111, 114, 124
Nixon, Tom  65, 154, 155

## O

objection  33, 79, 81
Ordinata  12-13, 27, 64, 75, 76, 94, 105, 106, 132, 150, 156, 160
- partners of Ordinata  76, 94
owner, ownership  18, 36, 46, 60, 107

## P

participatory dynamics  13, 75-81, 99, 109, 112, 132
passion  21, 34, 43, 53, 54, 60, 112, 118, 119, 136, 138, 151
pathology, source malady  42-54, 83, 86, 124, 130, 137
pathway  35-36, 74
personalist norm  159
photography  145-147
Plato  129, 158
power  20, 21, 26, 36, 44, 49, 68-69, 71, 80, 88, 90, 100, 107, 119, 122, 156, 157
primacy, principle of  80-82
purpose  35-36, 39, 74

## R

reciprocal causality of total causes  68, 156
recognition of source  42, 43, 44, 50, 75, 80, 85-95, 124
*Red Book* (Jung)  138, 159
Reed, Jane  151
reflection  13, 32, 33, 35, 36, 92, 93, 110, 112, 124, 152
*Reinventing Organizations*  77, 132, 154, 157
relationship  22, 28, 32, 42, 46, 48, 53, 59, 60, 61, 82, 83, 91, 92, 100, 102, 115, 126, 127, 136, 137, 157
representative of the source  125-126
reputation  28, 104
resonance  93
responsibility (of source)  36, 38, 42, 43, 44, 49, 52, 59, 60, 61, 62, 65, 66, 67, 68, 71, 77, 80, 83, 85, 88, 91, 92, 100, 102, 110, 112, 119, 124, 126, 132
- relative responsiblity  67-68
- shared responsibility  77, 85
- total responsibility  65-68
Revault d'Allonnes, Myriam  68, 156
risk  27-28, 33, 43, 44, 52, 61, 82, 83, 88, 91,

102, 104, 105, 110, 114, 123, 124, 126

## S

Sarthou-Lajus, Nathalie 100, 101, 102, 104, 111, 114, 115, 130, 157
self-confidence 28, 44, 48
slacker (source malady) 50-52, 53, 62, 124, 137
Smith, Karen 5, 149, 150, 151, 152
Sociocracy 132
soul of the project 35, 36, 39, 107
source-compatible 132
source denier (source malady) 42-46, 48, 49, 51, 53, 124, 137
source-donor 101, 102, 107, 112, 113, 114, 117, 119, 120
source economy 61
source-evolution interview 94
source malady 42, 64, 86, 119, 124, 137
source person 7, 17, 18, 20, 21, 22, 23, 25, 26, 27, 28, 29, 31, 32, 33, 34, 35, 36, 37, 38, 39, 41, 42, 43, 44, 46, 47, 48, 49, 50, 51, 52, 53, 54, 59, 60, 61, 62, 65, 66, 68, 69, 70, 71, 74, 77, 79, 80, 86, 90, 99, 100, 101, 105, 109, 110, 112, 115, 118, 119, 120, 121, 123, 124, 135, 136, 137, 153, 154
source position 53, 64, 68
source principles 11, 12, 13, 21, 22, 23, 46, 47, 54, 70, 87, 93, 100, 108, 125, 126, 129, 130, 132, 133, 136, 137, 138, 142, 149, 150, 151, 152, 153, 154, 155, 157, 160
source-receiver 100, 101, 104, 107, 112, 113, 114, 117, 120
source role 22, 26, 42, 44, 46, 47, 52, 87, 91, 92, 107, 108, 109, 114, 117,118, 120, 122, 123
source-usurper 48-49, 62, 69, 86
source vocabulary 12, 64, 87, 126, 132, 133
sourcework 142
space 31, 47, 60, 66, 68-69, 83, 114, 156, 157
specific source 20, 61-71, 73, 74, 75, 77, 79, 80, 81, 82, 83, 84, 85, 88, 90, 91, 92, 100, 104, 105, 106, 107, 113, 114, 121, 124, 126, 158
spirituality 137
Stallard, Tash 151
successor (receiver of source transmission) 38, 101, 104, 106, 110, 111, 112, 113, 115-119, 121-123
synergy 74, 76, 84, 91, 94

## T

Teal Organizations  132, 157
team  12, 43, 61, 71, 75, 79, 92, 106, 114, 152, 160
Thomas Aquinas  158
threshold  11, 18, 114-115, 155
time  66, 68
torch (of the project's source)  108-109
trainings on source principles  160
transmission of source  99-110, 111-115, 118, 119, 120, 121, 122, 129, 130, 157, 158
- failed source succession  107, 114, 119-121
- formal transmission  112-113
- horizontal transmission  100, 104, 105, 106, 113
- informal transmission  112-115
- non-transmission of source  108-109
- vertical transmission  100, 104, 106-107, 113
trust, confidence  28, 31, 47, 81, 101, 102, 105, 110, 114-115, 120, 122, 123
Twain, Mark  27
tyrant (source malady)  46-50, 53, 62, 69, 137

## V

values  22, 26, 36-39, 50, 52, 60, 61, 65, 67, 70, 74, 75, 76, 77, 80, 81, 88, 92, 93, 107, 109, 117-118, 124, 136
- personal values  37, 74, 92
- shared values  38
Vatican II  159
virtue  53
vision  22, 26, 29, 33, 34, 35-36, 38, 39, 50, 51, 52, 60, 61, 64, 65, 67, 70, 71, 74, 75, 76, 77, 79, 80, 81, 88, 92, 93, 107, 117-118, 119, 124, 136, 157

## W

«we»  76, 82, 93
Wojtyla, Karol  137, 158
workwithsource.com  12, 154, 155, 160

"Flowing to the sea, the river stays true to its source."

Jean Jaurès

*First English Edition*

*published on 8 September 2020*

Production and distribution by BoD—Books on Demand, Germany
and its international partners
on behalf of Aquilae Editions, Switzerland